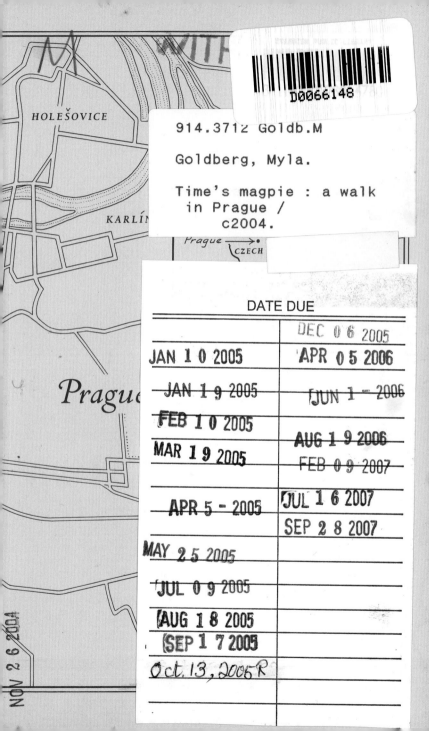

HOLEŠOVICE

KARLÍN

Prague ⟶ •
         CZECH

Prague

NOV 2 6 2004

Time's Magpie

Time's Magpie

A WALK IN PRAGUE

Myla Goldberg

ILLUSTRATIONS BY KEN NASH

CROWN JOURNEYS
CROWN PUBLISHERS · NEW YORK

Copyright © 2004 by Myla Goldberg
Illustrations copyright © 2004 by Ken Nash

Published by Crown Journeys, New York.
Member of the Crown Publishing Group, a division of Random House, Inc.
www.crownpublishing.com

CROWN JOURNEYS and the Crown Journeys colophon are trademarks of
Random House, Inc.

Printed in the United States of America

DESIGN BY LAUREN DONG
MAP BY JACKIE AHER

Library of Congress Cataloging-in-Publication Data
Goldberg, Myla.
    Time's magpie: a walk in Prague / Myla Goldberg.—1st ed.
(Crown Journeys)
    1. Prague (Czech Republic)—Description and travel. 2. Prague
(Czech Republic)—Social life and customs. 3. Goldberg, Myla—
Travel—Czech Republic—Prague. I. Title. II. Crown Journeys series.

DB2022.G65 2004
943.7 1205—dc22 2004016328

ISBN 1-4000-4604-1

10 9 8 7 6 5 4 3 2 1

First Edition

To Jason, who went with me, and to
Zelie, who came back with us.

Contents

You should travel to Prague when the days are long, so you will be rewarded by a fair view as the train crosses the placid River Vltava. . . . You have had your first glimpse of Prague, and it was beautiful, so you set about endeavoring to enter into the spirit of the place, to absorb its atmosphere and to study its character. For every ancient city that has stood up against adversity and overcome it has a very definite character of its own. And it is a mysterious and wonderful thing this character, this cachet of a great city. . . .

—B. GRANVILLE BAKER,
From a Terrace in Prague, 1923

*F*ORGET THE LONG DAYS. WHEN THE DAYS ARE long, bands of Germans and Italians and Japanese and British mob the narrow streets of Old Town, and herds of American college students in velvet jester hats and PRAGUE DRINKING TEAM T-shirts stampede across the Charles Bridge singing Pearl Jam songs. But in March or April, the worst of winter is over and the tourist hordes have yet to descend; by early September the summer crowds have dispersed. On the edge of a season it is still possible to duck onto a narrow, cobbled side street to find it deserted and to feel time straddling centuries the way Prague straddles its river. So many of Europe's cities have been bombed and burnt and torn down and rebuilt again that their physical history survives in stray fragments or not at all, but Prague is time's magpie, hoarding beautiful, eclectic bits from each successive era. In Prague, Gothic towers neighbor eleventh-century courtyards, which lead to Baroque and Renaissance houses with twentieth-century bullets embedded in their walls. Art Nouveau hotels abut formerly socialist department stores that now sell French perfume and American sneakers. Through a combination of luck, circumstance, and obstinance, Prague has stockpiled ten centuries of history.

The city's unrelenting profusion of stimuli forces the brain to screen things out, until one day a new sort of detail will ambush an unconscious filter and then appear everywhere, remaking once-familiar streets. Almost every city block displays a plaque commemorating Prague's countless martyrs from across the centuries—resistance fighters and outspoken nationalists, religious heroes and fallen soldiers. Usually these plaques are placed over doorways, or just above eye level on a building's edge. Small and made of dark, weathered metal, they are easily overlooked but upon noticing one the rest appear, Prague's long, sad memory emerging with each additional step. It becomes impossible to go anywhere without noticing more names; Prague becomes a city overrun by death. Then, the eye will be diverted from the funereal by an ornamental frog decorating a doorway, or a marble frieze of a violinist fronting an apartment building that was a music school a century before. It becomes apparent that almost every building is charmingly adorned—even in the shabbier neighborhoods lion heads roar above doorways or cherubs recline below windows. The memorial plaques fade into the background.

The nemesis of ornament, Prague's graffiti also exists at first as visual static, soft and persistent and easily glossed over. Spray paint crawls across delicate Art Nouveau façades; black tags mar eighteenth-century marble; names are keyed into granite landings and wooden windowsills. In the wake of the Velvet Revolution, graffiti has spread like mold along the city's edifices, leaving practically no surface untouched. Here, where old beautiful buildings are the default rather than the treasured exception to time's entropic rule—and where rich architecture belies an impoverished budget—it's impossible to safeguard everything. Freed from Communism's straitjacket, the entire city is now wrapped in scrawl.

But the beauty of Prague's youth almost excuses their penchant for vandalism. Preternaturally appealing creatures with sculptural faces, creamy skin, and long, supple limbs, they lean against buildings, cigarettes dangling from their lips. They sip slow drinks in cafes; they spill onto the streets in acid-washed jeans. They cultivate looks of boredom that highlight their full lips and Slavic cheekbones. Their attractiveness is alarming in its universality and in its disappearance at the earliest intimation of middle age. Prague's denizens breathe coal-laced air, drink polluted water, and live on boiled dumplings and pork cutlets, beer and cigarettes—a diet that generally allots a person only three good decades. Faces become haggard and loose-skinned; bellies grow and arms become flaccid; spines curve; strange lumps and moles appear.

In Prague there is no culture of continuing care facilities or retirement communities. The old are not shunted away, nor do they move to sunny locales with more golfing opportunities. Prague is home to stooped old ladies with necks crooked like canes, and old ladies with perfect posture. There are old ladies in sensible, square-toed shoes and old ladies with sagging pantyhose stuffed inside bright red Mary Janes, old ladies with large handbags and fuzzy wool caps they knit themselves, and old ladies in ratty fur coats. In Prague the blue-haired old lady is no less common than the violet-haired old lady or the scarlet-haired old lady—punk rock dye-jobs hallucinatory in their vibrancy, and which are still commonplace a decade after the arrival of Western cosmetics might have been expected to impose a certain refinement of hue. Sometimes old ladies are in the company of old men but mostly old ladies are alone, or with old lady friends, or with small, unfriendly dogs. Husbands die, and perhaps there is a small pension, but old ladies still carry baskets filled with groceries. They still make their painstaking way down sidewalks and hold their breath as they risk the first stair of a speeding escalator.

The velocity and intensity with which Prague's inhabitants age merely mirrors time's unlikely acrobatics from one city block to the next. A street frequently occupies two centuries at once. In the city center, a T.G.I. Friday's inhabits an eighteenth-century mansion; signs posted on elegant antique streetlamps display the word CASINO in Czech, English, Japanese, and Hebrew; a fourteenth-century boulevard contains a McDonald's, a Pizza Hut, and numerous discos, its sidewalk hucksters proclaiming the virtues of nearby strip clubs.

Prague's magpie instincts are not strictly temporal. The mad rush toward Westernization has resulted in a spectacular street mélange of consumer culture, international tourism, and incipient capitalism. In Old Town, a restaurant tout sports an oversized sombrero and a Mexican poncho on which are emblazoned the words PIZZA and FALAFEL, while a restaurant named Chicago advertises Mexican cuisine. A gaggle of schoolgirls squawks, in accented English, "We're from Belgium, mighty mighty Belgium . . . " their voices echoing through the streets. A flock of Japanese tourists photographs the clock tower from the opposite side of Old Town Square, their flashes impotent against the deepening night. Kerchiefed, thick-fingered snack-stand proprietors vend—in addition to the traditional sausages and fried cheese—a frozen treat called Rentgen, a fluorescent yellow Popsicle on a black skeleton-shaped stick, with a radioactive symbol on its wrapper. On a pedestrian plaza, a street vendor waves a crumpled piece of paper at a cop in desperation, blocking his briefcase of fake Soviet artifacts with his body. From a loudspeaker fronting a downtown bingo hall, a voice drones each successive number in a robotic monotone that suggests imminent death from boredom. At a tram stop, a stray mutt trots back and forth before a woman eating a roll until she feeds him some crumbs. Prague's human beggars opt for complete prostration, facedown on their elbows and knees, hands proffered in supplication, a square of newspaper tucked under their legs for cushioning, but the dogs have better luck.

In the years since Communism's demise, gambling has become as common as graffiti. Along neighborhood streets, twenty-four-hour *hernas* advertise the day's accumulated jackpot on digital street displays, while inside the door, catatonic men feed coins into slot machines. Off-track betting parlors inhabit every major subway station. It's easy to become disheartened. Hopefully, discouragement will cast the gaze downward to Prague's sidewalks. They are not concrete or slate, but marble mosaics that stretch from the city's touristed center to its most ordinary neighborhoods; they are part of the city's fabric, nearly daring to be overlooked. There are never more than two colors of stone to a sidewalk, but those colors change.

Sometimes the stones are gray and white, sometimes roseate and white, marble cubes the size of children's blocks forming patterns that shift, block to block, from diamonds to checkerboards to squares of varying size. Who decides the pattern? Is there a plan in a municipal building somewhere mandating which city block receives nesting squares and which lines of diamonds? Occasionally small piles of marble cubes rest beside a patchy sidewalk, waiting to be set in place by a sidewalk fixer in blue overalls. Oblivious to the street traffic, he will patiently tap each stone into place with a metal mallet and a bricklayer's hammer, his methods no different from the pavers of 1763. In the intervening years, empire has been replaced by Communism, which has been supplanted by capitalism, each passing era leaving its mark but not obscuring what came before. The sidewalks persist in their mosaic geometrics. Whether ruled by emperor or dictator or venture capitalist, Prague is simply too old and its habits too engrained not to remain faithful to itself.

Invisible City

PRAGUE'S MUSEUM OF COMMUNISM LIES ON A pedestrian shopping concourse a few blocks northeast of Wenceslas Square, steps away from a building that once housed Gestapo and then Communist Party officers before its post–Velvet Revolution conversion to an upscale shopping mall. Advertising for the Museum of Communism has taken over most of the city's subway escalators; each ascent and descent is accompanied by smiling images of the 1980 Moscow Olympic bear toting a machine gun or nested Russian dolls bearing sharp, menacing fangs, with the English words MUSEUM OF COMMUNISM printed beneath. It is no coincidence that the advertising campaign smells American: the Museum of Communism was opened by an entrepreneurial American expatriate who also owns a successful jazz bar. When the museum opened a year ago, the Czech press complained that the creation of such a museum ought to have been left to Czechs. The American jazz bar owner responded that the Czechs, after ten museum-less years, had blown their chance. The museum proclaims itself to be the only one of its kind in the world—a statement sure to inspire budding entrepreneurs expatriated across the former Eastern bloc to start museums of their own. Until that inevitable moment, however, Prague's remains unique.

The Museum of Communism shares the first floor of an elegant nineteenth-century building, which it shares with a casino. A sign on the building's stairwell directs all comers either left, toward the museum, or right, toward the card tables. The only Czechs who choose the former path are museum employees. These employees are exceedingly polite, speak excellent English, and are perfectly happy to sell, in addition to museum admissions, Lenin candles in a variety of attractive colors, Lenin paperweights, and reprints of Communist-era propaganda posters handily outfitted with English slogans for the convenience of their purchasers.

Considering Prague's nascent penchant for tourist traps—in recent years the city has inaugurated a Wax Museum, a Sex Machine Museum, and a Museum of Torture Instruments—the Museum of Communism is surprisingly restrained. An actual historian was employed in the creation of the museum's careful displays. These trace Czech Communism from its national inception in the 1920s to the disintegration of the Soviet empire, making no mention of the Czech Republic's extant minority Communist Party, which since 1989 has become rather touchy about its public image. Though whiffs of Western bias are detected in the museum's starry-eyed assertion that Radio Free Europe—and not, say, economic collapse—was a leading cause of the dissolution of the Communist regime, the exhibits strive toward cultivating an air of scholarship rather than polemic. Mock-ups of a Communist-era classroom, a store with sparsely stocked shelves, and even a secret police interrogation room are all tastefully done. What the museum neglects to mention, however, is that it actually serves as an antechamber to the real Museum of Communism, which is the city of Prague itself.

Communism is merely the most recent bygone era to accrue on Prague's canvas. Empire, monarchy, reformation, counter-reformation, nationalist revival, and fascism all coat the city like successive strata of oil paint. Over time oil paintings thin and fade, sometimes revealing earlier notions of the artist. The outline of a head previously placed at a different angle will sprout like a shadow from a painted neck, or the figure of a child will emerge within the contours of a basket now filled with potatoes. In the exuberant urban revisions inaugurated by the Velvet Revolution, much of Prague's Communist apparatus was dismantled, discarded, or painted over, but some pieces remain. Other bits peek through hastily applied overlays or can be sensed in the gaps their deposal left behind, voids the city has not yet managed to fill.

Communism's most enduring legacy lies underground. Prague's metro is composed of three lines that roughly bisect each other at Prague's center to form a sprawling, six-pronged subterranean constellation. The Communist conception of human nature may have been improvident but the Soviets were masters of subway construction. More than ten years after the dissolution of the Soviet regime, Prague's metro is much grubbier than it once was but as efficient as ever, providing its citizenry both a means of transit and a lasting refuge in case of nuclear apocalypse. The vertiginous depth of Prague's subway tunnels is certainly due in part to the river they are required to pass beneath, but the ever-practical Soviets very likely intended the Cold War–era metro stations to double as fallout shelters. The stations are cavernous, their floors marble, their walls covered with brightly colored metallic tiles, each tile dimpled like a giant, space-age ashtray. The perfectly round bore of the massive subway tunnels calls to mind drilling machines lifted from the most speculative of da Vinci's notebooks or the pages of a Jules Verne novel.

These profoundly subterranean stations are reached via epic, steeply angled escalators that plunge 150 feet underground. To minimize this distance, the escalators run at cartoonishly high speeds, making it easy to envision eyeballs or noses or hair being left behind as the escalator whisks away. To anyone accustomed to the steady plod of the American escalator, Prague's version feels thrillingly unsafe: the heart accelerates at each embarkation and the phrase "to ride an escalator" reverts to its original, early-twentieth-century meaning when mechanized stairs were reason enough to visit the downtown department store. Despite the escalators' demonic speed it still takes an awfully long time to reach or leave the surface, but to walk rather than stand is strictly for Sherpas. There is time for lengthy plot descriptions of complex novels on these escalators; there is time for intense philosophical debate. It is easy to imagine love affairs beginning and ending in the time it takes to ride from top to bottom. It is not uncommon to see someone sitting on an escalator step as they ride, elbow resting on knee, hand cradling chin, asleep.

Today, the sloping steel medians between Prague's up and down escalators are lined with metal studs. As late as 1993, however, the metal dividers were smooth, providing gleaming, uninterrupted slopes of lunatic speed to anyone reckless or rebellious enough to hoist herself over the handrail. Riding the escalator at least halfway before sliding down provided a ride that did not necessarily guarantee death or dismemberment and was extremely fun, if unambiguously illegal. Sliding down escalator medians—like speaking candidly or playing rock music—was forbidden under Communism, a system ominous enough to prevent generations of teens from exercising their hormonal mandate to defy authority. Communism cast a long and dark enough shadow that even in 1993, four years after the regime's demise, median sliding was still a rare behavior. Ten years later, authoritarianism's final defeat should be measured not in the profusion of shopping malls and McDonald's restaurants, but in the ubiquity of the metal studs that now line every metro escalator median, for these signify a deeper change: the lure of the most fantastic slides ever constructed finally became stronger than fear of state reprisal. The young and the reckless began to heed their call, and the metal stud was born.

The reform symbolized by the metal stud, however, is limited. The ghost of deposed regime still haunts the subway tunnels in the form of a subterranean secret police force established at the subway's inception. The undercover metro man is the authori-

tarian alternative to the turnstile. He resembles every-
body else and is impossible to detect until there's a tap
on your shoulder—and it's the guy in the battered
leather jacket, the one who looks like he's on his way
to meet his buddies for a beer. He's got a fleshy pink
face, thinning hair, and watery blue eyes. He's got a
badge, but it's so small that at first glance you may
think you have been approached by one of the city's
many vendors of fake Soviet artifacts. The badge
seems to have been manufactured from gold-colored
plastic and is much smaller than a legitimate badge
ought to be—authority should not fit so easily within
the palm of a hand. However, this man is no vendor,
and his badge's legitimacy can be intuited from the
grave panache with which he wields its dinkiness.
The badge means if you don't have a metro ticket,
you will pay.

No two metro men reveal themselves the same
way: perhaps they teach the rudiments at the academy,
but the little touches are their own. This one draws
out the moment, extending his hand palm downward;
then, with a twist of his wrist he reveals his ace, the
trick card he has been palming all along. This one's no
dramatist: he prefers a straight-ahead approach, the
badge already out and waiting. Sometimes the badge
is retrieved from a jacket pocket, or pulled from a
waistband like a gun. Sometimes it is revealed in the

flash of an opened overcoat, a publicly sanctioned form of exposure. At the next subway stop, the metro man marches his quarry onto the platform to collect their fines and every head in the car turns to watch: these are the ones caught passing notes during class; the ones caught fighting during recess; the ones suspected of harboring anti-socialist sentiments. The context of capture may change, but the moment of revelation is always the same, essentially unaltered from its childhood predecessors of Tag and Duck Duck Goose. Growing older does not provide escape, only a game with graver consequences. In the metro, *Tag you're it* becomes *Ticket please,* and escape from this stewpot must be purchased.

Perhaps he's the guy with the blue bulky jacket that needs laundering; perhaps he's got jowls and small gray eyes. Maybe the undercover metro man is your neighbor; maybe he's the man at the head of the platform. Maybe there *is* no metro man, at least not this time, but one can never be certain and so it is better to buy a ticket. To any citizen of the former Eastern bloc, such reasoning is crushingly familiar, and so—over a decade after the city's eager embrace of the West—the private inhibition against fare dodging remains. Perhaps one day a critical mass of ticket shirkers will be reached and turnstiles will bloom at the entrance to every station, but for now Prague's metro is not only Communism's most prominent physical legacy, but its most lasting psychological one, a living artifact of a past regime Prague prefers to think it has left behind.

Aboveground, Communist architecture dots Prague in crazy-quilt fashion, interposing austere stone or brick façades and numbingly functional expanses of concrete in the dizzying amalgam of architectural styles that define Prague's cityscape. Communist-era apartment buildings nestle next to Art Nouveau hotels. Atop the entrance to a municipal building, a blocky sculpture of a worker stares eye to eye with a creamy-skinned Art Deco sylph across the way. The Communist philosophy of architecture viewed building ornament as an opportunity for oversized agitprop; and so the exteriors of Prague's Communist-era constructions are host to kerchiefed peasant women displaying leviathan feet too mighty for shoes and wrench-wielding mechanics caught mid-pull in heroic battles with hex nuts bigger than human heads. Divorced from propaganda and regime there is something sweet about a rectangular relief depicting a man inflating a tire, or laying bricks, or cutting stone, or carrying a food-laden tray to a table. These architectural artifacts retain a seed of Communism's idealism, which after all is a philosophy that contains within its ruptured, rotting heart a beautiful if chimerical concept. There is something lovely about being surprised at a street corner by a terra-cotta relief of a man cutting cloth: we don't often think of tailors, but they are important. Prague abounds in these commemorations, tributes to the smaller functional aspects of everyday life, facets too often invisible and overlooked.

Like its work ethic, the public signage of Communism has also outlasted its politics, but this evidence—inscribed across shop windows and printed on awnings and street signs—requires knowledge of Czech or access to a Czech–English dictionary to uncover. Prague's store fronts are the most ubiquitous vestiges of this former era. In the United States these surfaces would proclaim their individuality: there would be Joe's Hardware or Sally's Beauty Salon, Lopez Groceries or Good Rise Bakery. In Prague, where commerce was state-controlled for decades, stores still declare themselves in a blunt, standardized manner antithetical to Western standards of commercialism. In Prague, all small corner groceries go by the sole name *potraviny,* which means groceries. Bread is bought at the *pekařství* (bakery), produce at the store whose sign reads *ovoce zelenina* (fruits vegetables), and meat at the store proclaiming *maso* (meat) above its door. Clothes are purchased at *Levna Móda,* a reasonably exotic-sounding name to an English-speaker, but meaning only "Cheap Fashion." International businesses have made large inroads into the city's center, bringing with them the kind of store name the West takes for granted, but in the outlying neighborhoods, the old store names remain. With a little more time and capital (changing a sign requires more than a changed ethos: it also requires cash) GROCERIES Martina will certainly become MARTINA'S GROCERIES, but for now a day spent running errands in the city still feels uncannily like entering a George Orwell story or a dystopic sixties-era BBC television series.

Many of Prague's streets also continue to bear the stamp of an obsolete system. Renaming public thoroughfares was an ongoing Soviet preoccupation from the time the Red Army entered the city in 1945. Streets were rededicated to war generals and Communist cultural and political icons; bridges and squares were renamed for Soviet military triumphs and army battalions. A particularly nice stretch of road along the Vltava River was rechristened *Gottwaldovo nábřeží* for Klement Gottwald, Czechoslovakia's first "Working Class President" and a loyal Stalin toady. In the wake of Communism's collapse, the Czechs were eager to reclaim their streets, but they soon discovered they had grown unexpectedly fond of some of the old names. So while in the months following the 1989 Velvet Revolution, any street with Communist connotations was rebaptized, not all of these renamings took. As anti-Communist fervor subsided, distinctions were made and—as can be seen by a close look at a current Prague street map—many Soviet-era street names were permitted to return.

The prodigals were often writers. To this day, Prague contains a *Puškinovo náměstí* for Aleksandr Pushkin and a *Gogolova* street for Nikolai Gogol, but *náměstí Maxima Gorkého* has been consigned to the cartographical dust bin. It would be nice to think that the retained street names were the result of a lengthy and passionate debate over which writers best represented the artistic ethos of the city, but Czechs are pragmatists: it is likely the streets named for Gogol and Pushkin were allowed to return due to their suburban locations, where they could exist without posing a threat to notions of Czech cultural identity, while Gorky remained banished due to his formerly central location in Old Town. This practical bent is evinced in the other Soviet hangers-on, which tend to be located in the city's more distant corners and include *Sibiřské náměstí* (Siberia Square), which, with its whiff of exile and gulag, is appropriately located at the far northwestern corner of town.

Some of the new names aren't up to their assigned tasks. *Náměstí Kinských* (Kinsky Square) is a case in point. Until 1991, the square was called *náměstí Sovětských tankistů* (Soviet Tank Personnel Square), because it displayed—in what might have functioned as the city's longest-held parking space—the first Soviet tank to enter Nazi-occupied Prague. As resentful as Czechs are of their captivity under Communism,

Russia's liberation of Czechoslovakia from the terror of the Nazis still resonates in the country's historical memory: to this day outside Prague's central train station, there stands a startling statue depicting a Czech resistance fighter passionately embracing his Russian liberator. While the tank in Soviet Tank Personnel Square certainly represented the military might that kept Prague under Soviet control, it also symbolized the ephemeral period in Czech history when the Russians were liberators and not oppressors. And so, two years after the ousting of the Communists, the tank in Soviet Tank Personnel Square remained, a symbol of Russia the Czechs seemed reluctant to abjure.

Then, in 1991, artist David Černý painted the tank pink. His action was greeted by its immediate repainting by the authorities, but Černý's statement so inspired the city that the tank was soon repainted pink—and not by Černý but by six members of the new Czech Parliament. Soon afterward the tank was removed to a military museum and the square renamed for the nearby Kinsky Gardens. Then in 2001, after a decade of vacancy, Černý proposed that the pink tank be returned to the empty square as a symbol of the progress the Czech Republic had made since 1989. It was a controversial idea. Some welcomed the prospect of the tank's return, seeing it as a fitting symbol of Prague's transformation, but when the Czech prime minister called Černý's proposal arrogant and ill-conceived, popular support for the project waned. Perhaps in order to head off further initiatives by Černý, the Czech government decided they needed to fill the square themselves.

The fountain that now burbles at the center of Kinsky Square is unmarred by a single stripe of spray paint. It is so new that workmen still dig at its edges and the park benches surrounding it are pristine. Jets of water encircle a disk of rock, which is bisected by still more plumes of water. These water plumes are still being adjusted, and like an adolescent trying and rejecting several outfits the morning of the first day of school, the fountain waffles between ostentation and humility as it runs through its various test patterns. The jets spurt to alarming heights, a trick done in sequence like a watery can-can, but after one cycle of this they die down to a flaccid burble and remain there. Even at its most anemic, the fountain enthralls the Czechs. The benches encircling the fountain are full of oglers, their expressions those of children who have received a new puppy. A mother takes several pictures of her young son standing beside the fountain, but she is no tourist: she lives here. The Communists were not big on fountains; fountains were impractical, water-wasting symbols of bourgeois values. The fountain in Kinsky Square not only doubles the city's fountain population, but it is the only one people don't have to pay to see. And so, though intended as a rebuke to Černý, Prague's ministers seem instead to have embraced him because, aside from a pink tank, there are few things further removed from the Soviet mindset than a fountain's decadent burble.

What Communist-era Prague lacked in fountains it made up for in statues. Statues are inevitably the first things to go in the face of regime change, but dramatic photos depicting toppled tyrants only tell half the story. Because every discarded statue leaves behind a pedestal. Pedestals can be small, unobtrusive things or, depending on the statue, they can be more complicated. When a statue is torn down, its pedestal does not necessarily follow: pedestal removal is more costly and labor-intensive. The low-lying pedestal that once held Prague's Lenin statue, for example, rises smoothly out of an isosceles triangle of polished marble. Uprooting this modest plaza would have proven expensive and unsightly, so when Lenin was given the boot the pedestal and its plaza remained, an inconspicuous wedge of stone tucked to the side of a blighted, oversized traffic circle on the northeastern edge of town.

The top of Lenin's pedestal bears a rectangular scar marking where his statue once presided, but this is the only rough patch on the marble plaza's otherwise smooth expanse. This makes it a novelty in a city brimming with cobblestones, the bane of the small wheel. And thus, the empty pedestal is a commodity of rare value to an urban creature Westerners take for granted but that Prague has only known since 1989: the skateboarder. The post-Communist blossoming of skateboard culture has resulted in Lenin's pedestal being tagged in thick black marker and claimed for a ramp, a modest, smooth-planed oasis in a city of unsuitable skating surfaces.

More conspicuous, and potentially more dismaying to the pedestal's former tenant, is the bright yellow tent that occupies the far corner of the vacant marble plaza. There is no telling how long this tent has resided here, nor how long it will remain. Though the skateboarders seem unfazed by its presence, they keep their distance. The tent is populated by young men and women wearing bright yellow jackets printed with the words VOLUNTEER MINISTER. Anyone who ventures within hailing distance of the tent's opening will be greeted by a cheerful young woman with an unremittingly intense gaze, who will employ every technique short of physical force to encourage entry. Those who step within will be brought before a giant photo of L. Ron Hubbard, at which point—if they listen very carefully—they just might hear the distant creak of Vladimir Ilyich Lenin turning in his tomb.

In retrospect it is not so surprising that Scientology should fill a void left behind by Socialism: one prophet simply blazed the way for another. Between the plaza's two current squatters, the proletarian skaters certainly would be more to Lenin's liking; the hypothetical meeting between V. I. and L. Ron suggested by this tent on this plaza evokes images of epic cataclysm, as when matter and antimatter are brought into contact. Upon reflection, however, Hubbard's tenancy here seems inevitable: nature abhors an ideological vacuum.

Further proof of this axiom can be found in Letná Park, a pretty stretch of green that occupies a cliff overlooking Old Town from the Vltava's northern bank. At the edge of this cliff stands a giant, motionless metronome. It rests on a massive plinth that is several stories high and is constructed from rough-faced marble blocks that resemble the ancient battlements of a historic fort. Outsized iron doors at its base suggest the crypt of a once fierce and powerful giant. The red metal arm of the metronome is fifty feet high and is frozen mid-tick, like the minute hand of a timepiece, between the 1 and 2 of a giant, invisible clock face. A plaque affixed to the metronome attributes its creation to "The Prague Society for a Universal Czechoslovakian Constitution," and dates its construction to 1991. But the pedestal not only clearly predates the metronome, it dwarfs it. Whatever preceded the frozen metronome was really, really big, yet nothing here hints at what that might have been. The gap in the landscape is as inscrutable as a photo from which a figure has been airbrushed out.

In fact, the plinth was commissioned by the Czech Communist Party to support a thirty-meter, fourteen-thousand-ton statue portraying Stalin leading a worker, a woman, a soldier, and a botanist into the glorious Socialist future. The behemoth took hundreds of workers five years to build. Carved into its base was Stalin's proclamation FROM THIS DAY ONWARD THE AGE-OLD STRUGGLE OF THE CZECHOSLOVAK PEOPLE FOR THEIR NATIONAL EXISTENCE AND INDEPENDENCE CAN BE CONSIDERED AS VICTORIOUSLY COMPLETED, which must have come as a huge relief to all those Czechs who—having outlasted the short-lived afterglow of Nazi ouster—thought they were once again subject to occupation.

Triumphant speeches were delivered at the statue's dedication in 1955, but neither Stalin nor his sculptor witnessed the ceremony: Stalin had died two years previous and the artist had committed suicide prior to the statue's completion. Within a year of the unveiling, Khrushchev had revealed Stalin's crimes against the Soviet people, leading chagrined Prague officials to conceal the dishonored statue in scaffolding. Though one bureaucrat suggested that the statue might be saved if Stalin could be sliced off its front and replaced with "an allegory—perhaps a woman holding a bouquet," in 1962 the entire statue was demolished. The monstrous pedestal, however, was too massive to be destroyed and so it remained as a mute witness to the passing of an age, an enormous parapet edged by broad, wide expanses of smooth, smooth marble waiting for Communism's fall. Waiting for the skaters to come.

The Stalin plinth is skater nirvana. The Lenin plaza is a mere marble toenail clipping by comparison, a skater kiddy pool. Spray paint tags cover most of the plinth's accessible surfaces, and on a sunny day the air is dense with the liquid sound of spinning skateboard wheels and the clatter of wood against stone. The plinth's steps are good for perfecting aerial skills: its smooth expanses are ideal for turns and spins. There are a few hacky sack players, a few teenaged girls with dyed hair and fishnets looking on, but here the skateboarders reign supreme. The few adults at the pedestal's expansive summit congregate near the metronome, away from the marble margins. The view from the metronome is excellent and it is clear why the plinth's designers chose this location: from here Stalin could oversee the castle, the bridges, and all of Old Town, as if he were a spoiled child who had just been presented the most marvelous model train set in creation.

The frozen metronome begs the imagination to envision a time before its tall red arm fell still. On sunny days, the metronome could have been set to a leisurely *andante* to encourage the city to slow down and savor the blue skies; on gray days the tempo could have been upped to a peppy *presto* to lift Prague from its doldrums. Concerts held at the base of the metronome would have required no conductor. Dancers whirling at its base would have always been assured of the downbeat. The connections between a giant metronome and a unified Czechoslovakia are murky at best, but by the time of the metronome's installation in 1991, a clear rift existed between Czechs and Slovaks. It would have behooved the Prague Society for a Universal Czechoslovakian Constitution to remember the history of the plinth they employed for their grand, cryptic gesture, for within two years of the metronome's erection, Czechoslovakia had divided itself into discrete Czech and Slovak republics and the metronome's tall red arm had mysteriously ceased to swing.

Letná Park's empty pedestal syndrome does not end there. The most recent personage to succumb to the plinth's siren call was Michael Jackson. In 1996, a ten-meter-high steel statue of Michael Jackson was erected near the metronome on Stalin's old pedestal—which shows once again the danger of leaving those things lying around empty—from which Jackson launched what has so far proven to be his last world tour. Today all signs of Jackson, like those of Stalin, have been thoroughly erased. Only Letná's oldest visitors remember the pedestal's original tenant. When they die, their memories of Stalin will die with them.

Library, Interrupted

ALONG THE TOURIST-CLOGGED ARTERIES OF OLD Town, a pizzeria advertises CHICKEN COVERED IN CORN FLAKES. A souvenir shop specializing in marionettes displays a puppet of an old Hasidic Jew beside a puppet of Harry Potter. Shoppers dawdle along the edges of the cobbled streets, scanning menus and fingering marionettes, trying on hats and debating the merits of Bohemian crystal, leaving the center of the narrow passageways to the city's more resolute sightseers, who forge down the dogleg streets that lead from Old Town Square to the Charles Bridge. Their path takes them past an unremarkable stone archway marked with a discreet plaque that reads NÁRODNÍ KNIHOVNA. The Charles Bridge lies mere steps away; the plaque is not in English; there is no reason to suspect the courtyard contains one of Prague's greatest time warps. Nothing about the archway or even the anonymous, multi-armed courtyard within betrays the presence of the National Library. Czechs already know where the library is: it's been in the same spot for over three hundred years. As far as they're concerned, there's no need for a tourist to be told.

The Czech National Library inhabits the extensive maze of buildings known as the Clementinum, which served as a Jesuit college until the Jesuits were tossed out in the late 1700s. The best way to locate the library is to look for the smattering of Czech college students intently smoking cigarettes outside its door, as the library is one of the very few places in the entire country where smoking is actually prohibited. The entrance itself, with its cracked plaster and its plain wooden doors, looks more like a modest college library than a national repository. There are no stone lions, no marble stairs, none of the trappings that earmark the famous libraries of great American cities. The foyer is small and beige and unprepossessing; the information counter could belong to any modest student union building. Past the counter two grumpy women staff the coat check, beyond which is the catalog room. Like any research library, the Clementinum's holdings can only be accessed piecemeal from closed stacks beyond the purview of visitors. But here, a visitor with an ID and twenty crowns (eighty cents) can procure a piece of white card stock the size of a pack of cigarettes, with their name printed in block letters below a bar code sticker and above a rubber stamp whose ink bleeds into immediate illegibility upon its application. That this charmless, flimsy object permits its bearer access to a vast collection of books older than the Pilgrims' landing at Plymouth Rock is tangible proof of the National Library's intrinsic powers.

Just beyond the entrance to the coat check, a uniformed guard sits sentry in a small booth that resembles the concierge desk of an old-fashioned hotel. Beyond are dusty glass cases displaying photos and pamphlets, once arranged with care by some anonymous staff person. Utilitarian light fixtures and an interior slathered in thick coats of institutional beige erase all sense that this was once a monks' cloister. There is no whiff of Jesuit here; the centuries have been painted over. As long as the gaze is fixed straight ahead this hallway could easily belong to an academic institution in Cleveland.

However, beyond the windows lining the hallway's left-hand wall, there is a square courtyard and while the hallway is clearly maintained on a regular basis, there is no sign that anyone has set foot within this courtyard since the Jesuits' expulsion. What at first glance appears to be a square of well-tended grass proves on closer inspection to be pale green moss that, in the absence of foot traffic, has overcrept the paving stones. At the center of the moss-covered square stands a dry fountain for which even the idea of water seems a distant memory. The stone of the fountain is dark with the accumulated soot of countless Prague winters. It may have been white once but there is no way to tell. The courtyard's walls crawl with leafless ivy branches thick and numerous enough to evoke networks of veins in a vast circulatory system, lending the architecture itself the air of an ancient hibernating creature. In such a setting, in a place where time's passage has taken on the sticky consistency of maple syrup, the painted solar clocks that appear between the thick swags of ivy feel absolutely contemporary: within this overlooked square of neglected moss and stone, no other timepiece has yet been invented.

Along the right side of the front hallway, the first door opposite the time-trapped courtyard leads to a room that was originally the Jesuits' refectory but which for over two centuries has served as the library's main reading room. The door that leads to the reading room is fitted with a medieval lock, its complex iron fittings stretching menacingly across the door's width. That the Jesuits were not the first to inhabit this place is made abundantly clear by this door, which could just as easily have been installed when the Clementinum served as Prague's headquarters for the Inquisition, four hundred years prior to the Jesuits' sixteenth-century arrival. It's the sort of door more commonly seen behind glass in a museum. The idea that it is meant not only to be handled but opened feels illicit, but the feat is easily accomplished, triggering no alarms, and then the reading room is revealed.

The library's reading room is much deeper than it is wide and is lined on one side with massive cathedral windows. Entering at one narrow end and gazing down the room's length, it is easy to picture rectangular wooden tables lined with hungry Jesuits, the air echoing with the sounds of priestly mastication. A few steps beyond the entrance, what looks like an eight-foot-tall ceramic funerary urn containing the ashes of the Inquisitors' unfortunate victims is in fact the very Rococo stove that warmed the Jesuits during the room's previous incarnation.

Just above the medieval door and its twin at the other end of the wall hang two small paintings, darkened and yellowed with time, that attest to the priests' continuing presence. Illuminated triangles contain an eye and an ear. The respective words OMNIA VIDET and OMNIA AUDIT are still clearly legible beneath the sense organs. Though the silence that reigns here is as potent and welcome as a familiar smell, appreciable to anyone who has spent concerted time in a library, there is an underlying sense of tension unique to this place, as if at any moment a robed monk might materialize to slap the back of a dozing neck with a ruler and grill the poor soul on the finer points of catechism.

Time's uneven passage in the reading room mirrors the flow of Old Town's teeming foot traffic: it progresses most quickly down the room's center and dawdles at the edges. The high, vaulted ceiling is so extensively frosted in stucco that it resembles the surface of an elaborate and eccentric wedding cake. Above the wall of windows, plaster reliefs depict angelic and mortal figures in varying degrees of agony, as if their forms are not decorative but load-bearing and after hundreds of years they aren't sure whether they can still manage the ceiling's weight. The ceiling cherubs are at first hard to distinguish from the dense rabble of ornamentation, but four of them appear at regular intervals along the ceiling's length, dividing the room into quarters. Each cherub hangs directly upside down and appears to be emerging, waving, from some sort of ornamental lettuce. Only one leg remains in the vegetable: the rest of the body dangles, one chubby arm outstretched in a frozen greeting that predates the American colonies.

Oblivious to the strange grandeur adorning the periphery, the middle of the reading room is occupied by a phalanx of utilitarian desks that wouldn't look out of place in a poorly endowed twentieth-century lecture hall. The timeworn beige and roseate flagstones that ennoble the floor's perimeter transform beneath the desk legs into ugly linoleum, creating the impression of a Versailles receiving gallery grafted onto an obscure Midwestern auditorium haunted by censorious priests. It's the sort of setting hastily supplied by the subconscious, in preparation for a dream about an unannounced exam and forgotten clothing. And yet, so much thinking has been done in this room over such a long period that the room's eccentricities achieve an unexpected harmony. The ugly desks assert their citizenship as firmly as the dangling cherubs, the room's unapologetic anachronisms providing a sanctuary beyond the incidentals of time and place.

Returning to the hallway and turning right reveals the rear corridor where the card catalogs begin. They are singly unimpressive—any one of them would be perfectly comfortable in a small-town library—but in aggregate they are breathtaking. The hallways of the National Library are long and narrow and its walls are one continuous line of card catalogs, a parade of wooden drawers fronted by handwritten labels. Though the National Library claims a modest inventory of computers, these are relegated to the catalog rooms, and even there they are dwarfed by the sheer number of card catalogs surrounding them. These cabinets are a reminder of how sensual a library can be. They attest to the perpetuation of a different kind of digital experience, in which fingers trace the length of a drawer rather than tap at a keyboard. Each catalog drawer, when opened, exhales the scent of old paper, a subtle interplay of dust and glue and wizened wood pulp. The cards vary: some are white cardstock, some are a pale mint green, and others are onionskin. Some are typed, some are mimeographed, and some are handwritten. Each moves beneath the finger with a subtly different gravity. Some have the softened, yellowed edges of frequent fingering, while others exhibit the crisp, unsullied corners of a hidden treasure. Though America has not wholly forsaken its card catalogs, they have become the doddering aunts of its libraries, burdens to be shouldered as lightly as possible so as not to detract from the computers that have replaced them. It's easy to forget that the data on those computers was entered by hand, each glowing catalog entry transcribed from a paper predecessor. The National Library's card catalog is the paper equivalent of Prague's mosaic sidewalks, in which the effort of a human hand is apparent in the placement of every paving stone. Hundreds upon hundreds of small paper rectangles nest inside each drawer, secured in place only by the past intention of the anonymous hand that once undertook their meticulous alphabetization. Time's slowed passage means that the National Library still relies on trust and not technology for its well-being. Its holdings have not been scanned onto microfiche, and its extensive catalog can be disrupted with the single, fluid motion of a hand yanking a drawer from its housing.

The library's resistance to the march of progress stems from a grim rather than romantic source: the National Library is in dire financial straits. The flood that struck Prague in the winter of 2002 was a disaster for the Library, damaging some of its most precious holdings and undermining its very foundation. There is talk of moving the entire institution to more stable ground, a massive undertaking for which funds are nonexistent. Meanwhile, the library remains where it always has, and water-logged volumes as old as the Clementinum itself have been flash-frozen inside rented meat lockers to stave off fungal damage. In the form of the lone watchman at his desk, the National Library's vulnerability becomes tangible. Until its fortunes improve, the National Library must persist in the hope that like its moss-covered courtyard, it will continue to find shelter in time's shadow.

The Noon Signal:
A Speculative Tale

THESE ARE THE AVAILABLE FACTS REGARDING THE Clementinum's Astronomical Tower: it is the pale yellow of butter pecan ice cream; the eight-sided cupola at its apex boasts a wraparound balcony with a gracefully curved railing and a Baroque statue of Atlas; the tower's windows are numerous, vary in shape and size, and include four that are perfectly round and vaguely nautical; for eighty-six years the tower was the source of Prague's noon. This last piece of data is supplied by a spare chronology of the noon signal, unceremoniously affixed to an inner wall of the tower, within a small chamber that serves as a museum for old astronomical equipment. Like so many of the best aspects of Prague this brief biography provides just scant enough information to ignite the imagination.

With modernity, noon has been reduced to a mere number, signifying but no longer representing the moment the sun reaches its zenith in the sky. Local accuracy has been replaced by global synchronization. Barely a century ago, however, noon was still determined by the sun, and in Prague it was determined in the Astronomical Tower's Meridian Room. The Meridian Room was a dark chamber with a small hole bored in its southern wall. A string ran across this room, representing Prague's meridian. When the sun's narrow beam passed through this hole and crossed the string, the sun had reached its zenith: noon had arrived.

By 1842 Prague had become a large and prosperous city with many bell towers, all purporting to ring in noon, but until then there had been no coordination of these bells, and so on the order of the High Burgrave of the Kingdom of Bohemia, a public noon signal service was begun. As noon approached on the morning of July 20, the city's bellmen observed as a flag was hung from the Clementinum tower. A few minutes before noon this first flag was replaced by a smaller one. When sunlight gilded the string in the darkened chamber below, the flag was withdrawn. The church bells rang. Noon had come to Prague.

The historical record states that the first noon signal was given by the director of the Clementinum's observatory, but certainly the director would have had more important things to do than give the signal on each subsequent day. It seems reasonable to assume that a regular signalman was retained, but the sparse history posted within the astronomical tower neglects to mention such a man.

According to a centuries-old legend the city's most illustrious rabbi, Rabbi Loew, once fashioned a golem out of Prague's clay. To create a signalman from ink, then, is a comparatively modest undertaking. Jiři lived in a small cottage in the Clementinum's shadow. A widower with a young son, Jiři did odd jobs around the Clementinum compound. He was a proud, meticulous fellow who dressed neatly, cleaned under his fingernails before every meal, and was scrupulously punctual. For twenty years, Jiři executed his tower duty with precision, never missing a noon. Though the signal flag was but one of Jiři's various functions, it was the only one he held dear. Standing atop the tower, feeling the eyes of the city upon him as he waited for the precise moment at which to withdraw the second flag, Jiři became a man of singular importance, a man upon whom all of Prague depended. His displeasure at the change imposed in 1866—when the two-flag method was determined to be too elaborate and noon's arrival was demoted to a single waving flag—would have been understandable. After twenty years of faithful service, to be demoted to just one flag! In tendering his resignation, Jiři would not have mentioned this indignity, instead offering the pretext of old age and the tower's winding stairs. After all, there was his son to consider, and while the signal tower had lost its former grandeur, noon was still a paying job.

The historical record does not explain why, toward the end of the century, a single cannon shot from the opposite side of the river was appended to noon's arrival, though logic suggests the city limits had expanded beyond the ability of Prague's more distant bell-ringers to view the tower's flag. No matter what the cannon's actual purpose it was likely resented by Jiři's son, who would have felt upstaged by the addition of artillery, recalling the affront his father had suffered two decades before. A cannon shot was imprecise. As it could be signaled only by the tower's flag, its retort would mark a lesser, retroactive noon, one that necessarily arrived on true noon's heels. Jiři Jr. would have balked at being party to such a distortion: he was a second-generation noon signalman with a reputation to uphold. The temptation to resign would have been great, but practicality would have trumped pride. Jiři Jr. was still young, with a family to feed; there was no guarantee a replacement would wave the flag with the crisp precision Jiři Jr. had learned from his father. To spare noon further degradation—and himself his family's dismay— Jiři Jr. would have remained.

The existence of such a son seems the easiest way to explain what happened next. In 1891 the time zone—a concept that originated in England—crossed the Channel. Across Europe, time became a gentleman's agreement: it was decided the continent would be divided into four regions, each with its own noon, Prague's coinciding with Vienna's and Berlin's. For obvious reasons, such a prospect would have deeply disturbed poor Jiři Jr. He, like his father, had pledged fealty to the Jesuits' string. His signalman's heart knew noon was non-negotiable. And so, when the observatory director issued the new decree, Jiři Jr. would have acquiesced without complaint. He would have agreed to follow the new procedure. And then he would have done what he had to do.

The modest printed page affixed to the observatory's interior states simply and without fanfare that for twenty years, Prague's noon trailed Vienna's and Berlin's by 140 seconds, remaining true to the moment the sun reached its zenith over the city. This sentence, hidden within an otherwise dry timeline, invites the reader to overlook its significance: for two decades a temporal insurrection was waged. There is no mention of the author of this revolution, no description of the daily battles that were fought. For twenty years Prague defied the rest of Europe and then—for reasons the thin chronicle fails to mention—

it stopped. In 1912, Prague's noon joined Central Europe's. The insurrection ceased.

Here is how it must have happened: for twenty years Jiři's son feigned loyalty to Greenwich but remained true to Prague's meridian. For twenty years he watched the string. It was a weighty secret to carry, the secret of a city's noon, but it would have been an easy one to keep. Time is too ubiquitous not to be taken for granted: to question it is like questioning the sun. When the signal flag waved, no one would have had any reason to suspect that their noon was late.

He died in 1912, when the stairs finally became too much. He died on the tower after the sun had reached its zenith, with the signal flag clutched in his hand.

Welcome to New Karlín!

THE VLTAVA RIVER WINDS THROUGH PRAGUE like a giant question mark, dividing the city into two halves joined by several bridges of which the Charles Bridge is the oldest, having spanned the river for over six hundred years. In August of 2002, the Vltava rose twenty-two feet over its banks, within forty-eight hours swelling to four times its normal size, birthing the worst flood the city had endured in over two centuries. River water poured through the streets of Prague, flooding medieval cellars and sub-way tunnels and submerging the ground floors of lower-lying neighborhoods. Cranes were rushed to the Charles Bridge to fend off waterborne debris before it assaulted the historic stone arches. Over fifty thousand people were evacuated from their homes as streets became canals. When the waters subsided, the damage to the city was estimated at over $2.83 billion.

The neighborhood of Karlín lies two miles north-east of the city center and just below the crook of Prague's liquid question mark. Karlín was Prague's first suburb, the nineteenth-century home of the city's manufacturing middle class. In the century to follow it devolved into a working-class neighborhood split between residential streets dotted with old, pretty buildings and former factories that once produced everything from trains and steam engines to hats. After the Velvet Revolution, gentrifiers envisioned reclaiming the neighborhood's middle-class roots: former factories were converted to office space; newly minted realtors spun Karlín as up-and-coming. Though Karlín could claim nothing noteworthy enough to draw the tourist crowd, it had aspirations of its own. This was before the flood.

Karlín's silence is more noticeable than its smell. The smell is a subtle thing, creeping into the forefront of consciousness only gradually, its familiarity at first fooling the brain. Karlín smells like an old basement after it rains, when water has seeped through the walls and up through the floor to take hold of the old couch and boxes of discarded books and magazines. The smell belongs to memories of rain-soaked tree houses and dank crawlspaces; it should not belong to an entire neighborhood. In Karlín, this smell hangs in the air like strange pollen from a water-choked flower. Gaping doors and glassless windows exude the scents of wet plaster and rotting wood, smells that combine to enclose the neighborhood in invisible decaying walls, imparting a sense of claustrophobia to even a deserted street.

Karlín's silence is an outright assault. The sound of Prague is the sound of its street traffic: the rubber burble of car tires against cobblestone, the screech of tram wheels grinding against the rails, the clomp of a babushka's heavy shoes against the sidewalk, and the murmur of manifold conversations. Six months after the flood's subsidence, the majority of Karlín's streets still remain closed to vehicles and there are no trains, the rails having collapsed along with the roads they traversed. Only half of the neighborhood's twenty thousand residents have returned to their homes. On a weekday afternoon, the sidewalks should be filled with women running errands and children returning from school; there ought to be old ladies waiting for buses. Occasionally a few stragglers appear—a woman walking her dog, a man sitting on a bench—but these lone figures only serve to magnify the neighborhood's emptiness. They are a reminder of all the other people who aren't here with them.

Even to a curious stranger for whom Karlín is a novelty and not a neighborhood, the urge to flee is strong. Karlín controverts some very basic urban assumptions. Histories of cities are read with a degree of wide-eyed wonder: it is difficult to envision a time when Manhattan was an uninterrupted expanse of green, when Rome was seven hills. The youngest of the world's great cities are found in America and these upstarts still assert themselves as foregone conclusions, even though the oldest among them are barely two centuries old. A city as old and retentive as Prague evinces its long history with the certitude of a natural formation. Its streetscapes impart inviolability; its buildings appear immutable. Such illusory notions play an important part in feeling at ease in a city. But in Karlín sidewalks are obstacle courses of metal barricades blocking off deep holes and piles of stones and mounds of earth. Decaying façades stretch from the pitted sidewalks to the archways of ground-floor doors and windows. Phone booths stand empty, gutted by flood. Most storefronts are still dark, gaping spaces, anonymous save for water-damaged signs over doorways indicating that here was once a jeweler, here a restaurant. Ugly sponge panels bandage damaged buildings, the batting meant to draw out dank water from flood-stripped exteriors. The sight of bandaged buildings adds to the sense of discomposure: buildings are not supposed to display wounds. In walking the ruined streets of Karlín it is impossible not to sense that one has entered forbidden territory. It is a sensation as old as childhood, the feeling one is seeing things one is not meant to see.

Devoid of inhabitants and window glass, a building's internal life becomes uncomfortably public. Because Karlín's apartment buildings are old-fashioned, high-ceilinged affairs, the river was unable to fully conquer their ground floors. Remnants of their antediluvian lives remain in thin bands along the rooms' upper edges. Through one gaping window there is a ragged stripe of parlor with a white archway and creamy yellow wallpaper. Through another is an ornamental plaster molding and a decorative chandelier, but below each of these narrow bands of normalcy, bare, crumbling brick walls descend from the tops of doorways to rough, cavelike floors. The violence of the flood lies in the jagged scar separating smooth plaster from raw brick, evoking a face from which not quite all the skin has been torn away. Building façades display the same uncanny ruptures, delicate Art Nouveau vines and thistles hanging incongruously above blasted expanses of stone and cratered brick.

Karlín's current populace is composed largely of workmen. Workmen in dirty overalls trudge past empty parks and closed schools and underneath a large banner strung across the front of a real estate office that reads, WELCOME TO NEW KARLÍN! Workmen emerge from dank entranceways and walk down ruined sidewalks carting wheelbarrows. Along a half-finished street, two men labor on their hands and knees pounding heavy oblong gray paving stones into place with metal hammers while two others stand beside them, wrestling successive stones into position with metal tongs. The sound of metal against stone is surprisingly musical. The hammers bang out a delicate two-note melody that comprises the only sound along the otherwise deserted street. The workmen do not walk the streets the way a resident would. It is clear by the way they carry themselves—their faces bored or tired or merely blank—that they have no connection to this place. To them Karlín is not a neighborhood; it is simply a broken thing they have been hired to fix.

Karlín's physical rehabilitation is slowly progressing. Streets are being reopened, buildings restored. Toward the end of March, the red X's that had obscured Karlín's metro stations on the city's subway maps since the previous August disappeared as if by magic. The reinstated stations are virginal in appearance, their surfaces free of scratches, dirt, and spray paint. They likely have not looked this good since the collapse of Communism over ten years before. Prague's other metro stations clamor with snack vendors, newspaper salesmen, and the occasional religious proselytizer. Teenagers loiter near phone booths; young mothers buy their children candy. The Karlín metro stations are empty of crowds and commodities. Their few patrons move quickly and silently from the trains and up the escalator to the empty street outside.

There is talk of people moving back. Whether encouraged by political forces or by their own predilection for underdogs, Radio Prague is fond of airing optimistic pieces proclaiming Karlín's beauty, historical importance, and ideal location. These pieces neglect to mention that Karlín lies on a flood plain, that most of its buildings were uninsured, that their owners lack the money for repairs. Under duress, a city like Prague, richer in history than in pecuniary assets, is necessarily forced to stage selective rescues. When the river rose cranes were rushed to the Charles Bridge—Prague's foremost symbol of urban immutability—fating Karlín to become an urban portent, a small persistent question mark lying in the crook of a much, much larger one.

The Museum of
Monastic Technology

THE DISTRICT OF HRADČANY LIES IN THE
shadow of the Prague Castle, across the river and
to the northwest of city center. Perched on a hill that
provides a dreamy view of the spires and domes of
Prague's cityscape, Hradčany epitomizes Prague's wonderful duplicity, in which dazzling charm exists within
a hair's breadth of eye-goggling eccentricity—for hidden within this quaint, quiet neighborhood of cobbled
squares and sixteenth-century cottages are the Strahov
Monastery cabinets of curiosity.

Strahov's only official attraction is its library. The
photo that lures tourists from the monastery's nonde-
script courtyard depicts a bibliophile's wet dream of
room. The walls are lined with densely ornamented
Rococo bookcases two stories high, which house a
collection of over forty thousand books more than six

centuries old. The ceiling is adorned in eighteenth-century fresco, and a red carpet along the wood inlay floor beckons in silent invitation. The one library feature that the photograph overlooks is the rope that stretches across the room's entrance, rendering the books, the shelves, and even the red carpet off-limits. Strahov's library rooms are arrayed like meticulously prepared corpses, their coffin lids opened to permit cautious viewing. Prague finds peculiar pleasure in teasing book lovers this way—the Clementinum also brags of a Baroque library but then doesn't permit paying visitors past the red velvet ropes barring its threshold. It is sheer bibliophilic cruelty to refer to such sepulchers as libraries. *Library* implies interaction with the books it contains, even if one's intercourse is limited to reading spines and inhaling the room's intoxicating must.

The hallway leading to Strahov's sequestered library is dimly lit and carpeted in ugly brown linoleum and discourages an extended stay. Its contents—a coat of chain mail and a coat of armor, a family tree of Francisco I, a wood-inlaid breakfast tray featuring Christ feeding lambs, two tinted pictures of an ancient and forgotten siege, and a diorama depicting the life cycle of the silkworm—might easily inhabit the drafty hallway of an Old World hotel that had been forced to pawn its nicer furnishings.

Dispersed among these haphazard objects are several antique display cabinets. Made of warm-colored wood and fronted by ornamental window-paned doors, they're nicer than anything else in the hallway, but their charms are modest in comparison to the spectacular bookcases in the adjoining library. At first glance the cabinets' contents are similarly uninspiring. Most are devoted to a collection of bird nests, shells, butterflies, and beetles. The shells are arranged in dusty rows that betray the uneven surfaces on which they were placed, gravity and time having worked in slow, steady tandem to make curves of straight lines. There are no signs, plaques, or explanatory literature, and the surly Czech matrons serving as security guards are equally unforthcoming. Officiousness is one pre-glasnost keepsake Prague is loath to disown—it is one of the few pleasures working-class Czechs can still afford. The matrons' position has granted them exactly two advantages over the tourists they've been hired to watchdog, and so their energies are divided between the scrupulous examination of each entry ticket and by the frequent excursions in and out of the barred library rooms.

Though the history of Strahov's cabinets of curiosity is muddy, the rare guidebook cites their establishment sometime during the eighteenth century. Perhaps the monastery's collection was once a grander thing but today it has been reduced to eight cases. The two most visible cabinets lie on the path between the two library rooms. One contains insect specimens. The other contains pottery, a china plate, metal stirrups, two china figurines of musicians in torn and dirty clothing, a knife, several harpoon tips, a lady's fan, two large cameos composed of tiny shells, an obscure map of interlocking terrestrial and celestial circles, and a three-dimensional crucifixion scene that has been assembled inside a glass bottle. The absence of documentation—in Czech or any other language—is disconcerting. Perhaps the pottery was excavated from beneath the home of a fifteenth-century count. Perhaps the china plate was once used by a Habsburg emperor, the metal stirrups by King Wenceslas himself, but there's no way to know. Tourism is funny that way: it's dependent on proper labeling. There is only so much time in a day and people want to make sure they see the important stuff—they haven't traveled halfway around the globe to look at Granny Horkova's favorite plate for serving cabbage. In the absence of information it is much safer and time efficient to move on to the next sure thing, and that's what most people who come to Strahov do: they peer into the barred library rooms and then they leave.

The hallway's two taxidermy cabinets face each other at one dim end of the hallway, where they are easily overlooked. Crabs, lobsters, and a turtle take up most of the space of the first cabinet. Small sharks, a crocodile, and a manta ray are among the inhabitants of the second, their arrangement reminiscent of a small-town natural history museum. The Czechs being a landlocked people, it seems reasonable to view these two cabinets as eighteenth-century precursors to the contemporary aquarium, their contents addressing intellectual limitations imposed by geography.

Twenty-first-century eyes know crabs and turtles. Presented with their familiar outlines, a twenty-first-century brain can supply the smaller details without deeper scrutiny. Strahov's Premonstratensian monks were reputed to be a respectable bunch—celibate, honest, and hard-working. The fresco on their library's ceiling is titled *The Struggle of Mankind to Know Real Wisdom.* In such a monastery, in the antechamber of one of Bohemia's most important book collections, the instinct is to trust. And so it would be understandable to accept that the crabs are crabs; the turtles, turtles.

The turtle that dominates the first cabinet is rather handsome. Its deep-brown shell is the size of a human torso and is impressive enough to upstage the four legs protruding from it. But the legs really deserve a closer look. They are slender and serpentine and delicate and to imagine them propelling the massive shell from which they emerge is to imagine a very special turtle. The legs are covered in thick black scales the diameter of silver dollars, the scales edged with real gold, with real gold spots in their centers. The legs end in feet with slender, five-clawed toes, the kind seen on antique bathtubs.

Below the turtle are three ostrich eggs nesting inside wicker baskets. Draped over one of them is an oblong fossilized specimen. The Czech label beside this egg is one of only two attempts at exposition within the taxidermic collection or, for that matter, the entire hallway. It helpfully translates: THE JESTERKA LIZARD SUCKS OSTRICH EGGS. While the length of the fossilized body is certainly suggestive of a youngish lizard, in lieu of legs it has fins. Perhaps the bulk of each leg was broken off in the young Jesterka lizard's struggle to suck out the insides of an egg so much larger than itself. The only other label in the collection decorates a glass jar containing a long, desiccated eel-like creature the color of bleached bone. AMERICAN SWORDFISH, the label translates.

The crown jewels of Strahov's collection—two creatures who glare at each other from their opposing cases across the hallway—also lack proper labeling, but their striking forms beg recognition. There's no historical evidence to support the notion that Lewis Carroll ever visited Prague but here—tucked within a quiet, overlooked corner of Strahov's monastery, secreted among the crabs and lobsters—are a bandersnatch and a jabberwock. The flattened bird head of the yellow-eyed bandersnatch emerges without benefit of a neck from what appears to be a large, over-stuffed sofa cushion fringed on two sides by a continuous fin, and ending in a tail that resembles a horseshoe crab's. Lacking any apparent means of self-propulsion, the creature likely floated on the water's surface like a jellyfish, waiting to devour unsuspecting children. It would have made mincemeat of the egg-sucking Jesterka lizard.

The jabberwock is the crown jewel of the cabinets. Measuring eighteen inches from the top of its crest to the tip of its tail, it is presumably a juvenile, the subject of the eponymous poem being considerably larger. Strahov's version has the legs of a duck and three sets of aquatic winglike appendages that only vaguely resemble skate wings. Its tail is segmented, as thick as a man's middle finger, and twice as long. Its scrawny neck is topped by the head of a malevolent Muppet, with a mouth that is not quite beak and not quite lizard's maw, open in mid-squawk. The top of its head sports a thicker, larger version of a rooster's comb, and from its right eye socket stares a baleful blue eye. The left one is missing: perhaps it was poked out by the bandersnatch before the two were separated. It's hard not to feel hopeless love for this ugly, impossible, overlooked animal. It's hard to refrain from building a jabberwock hutch for it in a quiet backyard somewhere, from feeding it chicken soup and consoling it with soft lullabies. In return it would certainly squawk and bite and shit all over everything. It would make an even worse pet than Strahov's stuffed armadillo, but clearly it had the monks under its spell. For two centuries it has received their benevolent sanctuary.

The monks who amassed this collection are long dead and their replacements remain beyond the purview of the paying public. If the postmenopausal Czech ladies who monitor the hallways know anything about the creatures in the cases, they're keeping it to themselves. And so, Strahov monastery presents an opportunity for an entirely different type of tourism, a mode of sightseeing easily transferable to the rest of Prague, where for every designated spectacle there are at least three that have gone unmarked and unsung. The anonymous inhabitants of Strahov's glass cabinets pose as many questions about their exhibitors as they do about themselves, questions the stately tomes amassed in the neighboring rooms cannot answer. Perhaps the monks were duped by the wily, worldly peddlers of taxidermy who darkened their door: after all, citizens of earlier centuries had the luxury of believing in a wider range of creatures than we jaded inhabitants of the twenty-first. But, perhaps, mixed with the monks' credulity was an equal amount of delight—perhaps they welcomed visitors to their cabinets with arched eyebrows and grandly outstretched arms. Perhaps late at night they gathered before the gold-scaled turtle, the egg-sucking lizard, the jabberwock, and the bandersnatch and giggled like mischievous children. In the absence of labels, anything is possible.

Political Theatro

OLD TOWN SQUARE LIES AT THE VERY HEART of the *Stare Město* district. For eight centuries, the square served as a marketplace, rows of merchants' stalls filling the cobbled plaza. Today the square is dominated by an Art Nouveau monument to Jan Hus, fifteenth-century Czech religious martyr and a celebrated symbol of Czech nationalism. The monument serves as a convenient meeting place for tourists and as a focal point for buskers and souvenir hawkers. Cafes and shops the pastel shades of after-dinner mints line the square's periphery. Their Baroque roofs are interrupted at one end by the Gothic tower of a thirteenth-century bell house and at the other by an ornate fifteenth-century astronomical clock that every hour unleashes a mechanical morality play from two cuckoo-clock windows.

Over the centuries, Old Town Square's size and location has made it an epicenter for celebrations, cataclysms, political enunciations, and executions. In the fourteenth century, King Wenceslas threw massive parties on the cobbles once the market had closed for the night; in 1600 the square was host to the world's first public dissection of a corpse. The square was the headquarters of the Resistance during the 1944 Prague Uprising, in which five thousand Czechs died in four days of fierce fighting against the Nazi occupation of the city. In 1948, a time when the Communists were still popularly viewed as the country's liberators, massive crowds gathered here to hear the words of Czechoslovakia's first Communist president. Compared to such events, the antiwar protest that occurs in the week preceding Bush's invasion of Iraq merits barely a faint parenthesis in the square's long history.

Turnout for demonstrations in Prague these days is generally slim; public dissent tends to be organized by the anarchists and the Communists, groups most Czechs want nothing to do with. At the appointed time of the antiwar rally, fewer than ten protesters are in evidence. They stand to the left of the Jan Hus monument, holding hand-painted signs. A young American woman in a bright orange NO BLOOD FOR OIL T-shirt distributes Czech information sheets to native passersby. She explains to the scant arrivals that they are early: the protest is not scheduled to start until two. The first antiwar rally was held three months ago and they are still tinkering with starting times.

The square is filled with tour groups and hawkers of marionettes, cheap jewelry, and glass. A few feet from the fledgling protest, a five-piece band is playing jaunty jazz standards. An American tourist interposes herself between two of the protesters so that her husband can snap a picture. If the woman could read Czech she would know that the sign being held by her photo op translates as AMERICAN AGAINST THE WAR, but the expatriate American protester is either too obliging or too embarrassed to spoil the couple's documentation of genuine Czech counterculture. After the husband snaps the shutter the couple heads toward the astronomical clock.

A small hatchback drives into the square and unloads an amateur sound system, several painted placards, and a skull-headed effigy wearing an I LOVE USA T-shirt and an Uncle Sam hat. A man with a gray moustache, wavy gray-streaked hair, and dark sunglasses distributes flyers for a post-demonstration demonstration sponsored by the anarchists, to be held four blocks away. His donation jar reads, INTERNATIONAL PEACE MOVEMENT OF THE CZECH REPUBLIC. He assures the assembled that a large group of anarchists and women against war are on their way. When a group of young people appears wearing black jackets, Che Guevara T-shirts, Palestinian head scarves and waving red flags that read Revolution, it seems safe to assume from the chaotic jumble of leftist fashion statements that the anarchists have arrived.

The jazz band breaks down their gear and recorded music starts playing through the small speaker set up near the hatchback. It is a strange medley: an old Chumbawamba tune is followed by reggae and then Latin music, all a little too distorted to be heard clearly. An elderly Czech woman walks by and is offered an informational handout. She already received a pamphlet, she answers; though against the war, she is resigned to it. "It's money," she shrugs, and walks away. Václav Havel, the national moral authority and until recently the Czech Republic's president, is an enthusiastic supporter of invasion. Other officials are less avid, but having sent a thirty-five-member team of biological, chemical, and nuclear decontamination experts to Iraq, the Czech Republic qualifies as a member of Bush's "Coalition of the Willing."

Czech posters begin appearing at the base of the Jan Hus statue as more people arrive. An American expatriate clutching a homemade English-language sign looks for someone to hold it; her group has made extra. Later, a septuagenarian gentleman and a middle-aged woman with violet hair can be seen standing behind English signs more than half their height, each sign bearing the distinctive hand-lettering of the industrious American expatriate. It is unlikely the couple can decipher the slogans they are promoting: most of Prague's older generation do not speak English. The couple peers into the distance looking stoic and long-suffering while pretending not to notice the few press photographers who honor their bid for a spot in tomorrow's newspaper.

By two o'clock, around two hundred protesters have gathered, a crowd reportedly twice the size of the previous rally. Though there are a fair number of American expatriates, the diverse crowd is largely Czech. There are young punk rockers and senior citizens, men in suits and men in leather jackets, women in torn jeans and women in knee-length skirts, all waiting quietly and patiently for the speakers to begin. Among them there is no bongo drumming, no chanting, no dancing, no puppets, none of the usual trappings of American protest. Perhaps the lack of excitement can be traced to the lack of policemen: there are only five in evidence. They stand at the edge of the crowd, looking bored. At American protests, one can rely on a large enough police presence to be assured one is behaving in at least a slightly brave or dangerous manner, but these police act as if there is no difference between the protesters gathered near the monument and the tourists waiting for the astronomical clock to chime the hour. Such authoritative apathy is distinctly enervating.

Finally, the protesters are provided a focal point: a young man climbs the tall base of the Jan Hus monument and unfurls an anarchist banner. Three of the policemen walk to the monument's base to request that he remove the banner and alight from Jan. From his perch the young man unleashes a dramatic physical and verbal tirade weirdly out of place beside the quiet crowd and the reggae soundtrack. When the young man eventually descends, obligingly taking his banner with him, the police try to escort him away but he refuses to cooperate, and so the foursome stalls at the leftmost edge of the statue, attracting a crowd of onlookers. The police convene for a hushed conference, leaving the young man sitting frozen in place before a clutch of curious spectators, resembling a child who has just thrown a tantrum in the produce aisle.

The American woman in the orange T-shirt opens the rally by asserting that the disruptive, banner-wielding, Jan Hus–mounting young man is in no way associated with the protest. Various speakers continue for a little less than an hour. A few try to initiate chants, but these never take. There is often applause and occasionally a shout of affirmation, but for the most part the crowd is attentive and appreciative, but staid. Most among the crowd are old enough to remember the Velvet Revolution; some are old enough to remember Prague Spring. Less than one hundred yards away, a memorial cross made of charred wooden beams commemorates the anti-Nazi fighters who died in the square in 1945. By three o'clock the rally has ended. A march toward the Mánes Bridge and the British and American embassies commences and the area surrounding the Jan Hus statue is once again empty, save for a few abandoned protest posters leaning against its base. Toward the opposite end of the square, the astronomical clock chimes the hour, unleashing its own five-hundred-year-old procession.

The war begins three days later. It is evening in Prague when the first bombs drop on Iraq, and by the following morning signs have appeared all over the city urging people to gather that evening in protest at Wenceslas Square. The half-mile-long boulevard was originally built in the fourteenth century as a horse market; now its shops and hotels serve as a crash course in nineteenth- and twentieth-century architecture. Art Nouveau, Cubist, Functionalist, and neo-Renaissance structures stand in unlikely cohabitation, beautifully ornamented façades neighboring blocky Communist buildings and post–Velvet Revolution constructions.

At the head of the square stands a large equestrian statue of King Wenceslas. Erected in the same decade as the Jan Hus monument, it is one of Prague's most symbolic sites, having served as a historical staging ground for a century of tumultuous events. The king and his horse witnessed Czechoslovakia's declaration of independence in 1918, when thousands of Praguers filled Wenceslas Square to weep with joy as their first president announced the formation of the fledgling country. In 1938, the statue looked on as Czechs denounced the Munich Treaty, which offered up a piece of Czechoslovakia to Hitler in a futile gesture of appeasement; a year later, a staged rally would signify the arrival of Nazi fascism. Wenceslas Square was the place where throngs of student protesters were met by brute force during the country's abortive and tragic attempt to temper Soviet totalitarianism in 1968, during which an eleven-year-old boy was shot dead on the steps of the statue as he pushed a Czech flag down the barrel of a Soviet tank. A year later, a Czech college student named Jan Palach became a national martyr when he burned himself alive here in protest of the Communist occupation; eight hundred thousand Czechs joined his funeral procession when it filed past the statue a week later. When Václav Havel was still a dissident, he was arrested for placing flowers by the statue in commemoration of Palach's death, and when the Soviet Union crumbled in 1989, Havel stood before more than a quarter million Czechs who filled the square to witness Communism's demise.

It is difficult to imagine Americans turning out in force in their own capital to protest the actions of another country, but the crowd that gathers here is fairly impressive. Many of the hallmarks of Sunday's protest are present: there's the same Uncle Sam effigy, the same flag-waving anarchists, and the same orange-shirted American woman who, when her turn arrives at the microphone, speaks at length in English about American dissent and recites a statement made that morning by Senator Robert Byrd, a speech incomprehensible to the majority of those assembled. That this crowd outnumbers Sunday's is certainly due in large part to the war's commencement, but the protest's more central location is also helpful. Most Czechs have no particular reason to visit Old Town Square and its gaggles of tourists, but Wenceslas Square is where Czechs work and shop, and it seems likely that a number of today's protesters happened upon the event on their way home from school or the office.

Several among the crowd have enlisted liquid assistance to combat the evening's bitter cold. A young punk rocker chugs from a cardboard carton of red wine, which he attempts intermittently to warm with his vigil candle. To his left, three men pass around a plastic soda bottle filled with an unappetizing milky liquid and yell in a slurred fashion at various inappropriate moments during the speeches. Spurred by varying combinations of indignation and alcohol, the crowd this time is chanting and calling out, and as the speeches progress there is even the beat of a lone bongo drum.

One man somehow manages to mount the unaccommodatingly tall pediment of the King Wenceslas statue to lean against the leg of the horse, where he stands making a V-sign with his fingers until he is asked by policemen to get down. Though the man seems willing enough, his inebriation has given him all the agency of a treed kitten. The assistance lent him by the police is patient and assured and it is clear now that a primary police responsibility at Prague rallies involves the disengagement of protesters from surrounding statuary. Though there are more policemen here than were apparent at the previous protest, they can still be counted on two hands. With the crowd growing to five hundred strong, it seems thrillingly possible that this time the police have miscalculated.

There is excited talk of a march to the U.S. Embassy. No official permission has been obtained for such a march and it is unclear, when the speakers conclude, whether this will be allowed to occur. Perhaps it is permitted because it can't be prevented: there are simply not enough police for the job. But as the march begins, it becomes clear that the police know their populace after all, for as the marchers swell down the length of the square they obligingly stop at each intersection to allow cars to pass. To an American eye, there are not nearly enough uniforms to enforce this politesse, but perhaps history has made Czechs cautious. Perhaps in a country where disobedience has so often been met with brutality, the stakes must be high to inspire anything but careful dissent. As the crowd proceeds down the length of Wenceslas Square curious tourists, shopkeepers, and club touts briefly stop what they are doing to watch; for a moment the orderly procession of sign-toting protesters is the best thing going amid the movie theaters and hotels, oversized billboards and garish signs advertising fast food and discos. Midway down the boulevard stands a young woman clad in a bright yellow jacket that reads: EROTIC THEATRO 44 NUDE. She has abandoned her post to watch the action, her handful of flyers momentarily forgotten. Then she too grows bored of the parade.

Ped Trap

MALÁ STRANA IS A GORGEOUS PRESERVE OF Baroque architecture ideally suited for aimless, daydreamy excursions down its narrow, winding streets. If one isn't paying close attention while ambling along a certain scenic avenue, it is entirely possible to end up following a narrow strip of sidewalk into a particular covered passageway just wide enough to accumulate trams. Once inside this passage the sidewalk disappears and is replaced by a small niche into which one must shrink to allow a streetcar to pass. On a sunny afternoon while rambling through Malá Strana, I emerged from this passage to find two policemen facing me as though we'd planned to meet. I smiled and continued to walk but they gestured for me to stop, pointing to a sign depicting a pedestrian diagonally bisected by a thick black line. I smiled and in my broken Czech thanked them for pointing out the sign and assured them that in the future I would be more careful. Until that point it was an interchange that could have happened in any number of American or Western European cities, the sort of benevolent policeman scenario found in stories written for children. Such stories are not written in Prague.

A first-time visitor to Prague might be led to assume the city possesses, along with its capitalist shopping and dining options, a Western European police force, but the Westernization of Prague's commercial sector does not extend to its cops. Prague's policemen are poorly paid and poorly trained and the majority are interested in using their position in whatever way they can for personal or material gain. Among Czechs, the police have a reputation for corruption, racism, and incompetence. Uniforms and guns earn compliance, but not trust. A policeman's actions are arbitrary and can shift according to any number of variables including but not limited to his mood at the time; the gender, general attractiveness, and nationality of his offender; and the weather. Most Americans, of course, have little reason to suppose the words and deeds of a uniformed police officer might not be based on a solid legal foundation. Coming from a country where corrupt cops are the stuff of national scandal, Americans are a largely trusting and compliant bunch, secure in their belief that police are, in aggregate, interested in protecting the citizenry from bad guys and maintaining order. In Prague, one comes to realize that certain basic American premises like accountability are, in fact, luxuries. Prague's police force finds this misapprehension extremely profitable.

The two policemen I encountered in Malá Strana that day were young, thickset men resembling soccer hooligans who had somehow scored *městská policie* uniforms. In Prague, the *městská policie* serve as the city's traffic cops, an echelon below the *obecni policie* who stand around looking bored at the periphery of political demonstrations. In place of the *obecni policie*'s more martial hats and coats, the traffic cops wear baseball caps and black canvas jackets stamped with the words MĚTSKÁ POLICIE. It was a warm day and the younger of the two *městskás* had unzipped his coat to reveal a black knit MĚTSKÁ POLICIE sweatshirt as well, the letters integrated into the weave of the fabric in the manner of an inexpensive sports team jersey, the kind given away to the first ten thousand spectators to arrive at a game. Perhaps it was the cheapness of the sweatshirt that clinched it, or my knowledge of the grievous state of Prague's police force; perhaps it was just that the afternoon was too lovely and my misstep too small, but on seeing the sweatshirt I envisioned

MĚTSKÁ POLICIE undershirts, sweatsocks, and boxers—
and the mental image of my antagonists with the
words MĚTSKÁ POLICIE emblazoned across their asses
made it impossible for me to take my situation seri-
ously.

Just as the interior of a Prague taxi furnishes no
information about the cab or its driver and therefore
provides no defense against being ripped off, the
Prague police uniform exhibits neither name nor
badge number. Not only does this make lodging a
complaint impossible but it forces me to invent names
for my two Malá Strana companions. I'll call the taci-
turn one Dim, for his alarming resemblance to Alex's
droog in *A Clockwork Orange,* and the younger, talka-
tive one The Mole, for the round black birthmark on
his left cheek.

Dim and The Mole were extremely pleased to
have stopped me; perhaps I was the day's first quarry,
or perhaps they particularly enjoyed detaining female
tourists. In any case they smiled like schoolboys who
had just scored a hall pass. I would need to pay a fine,
The Mole informed me, which was Dim's cue to
request identification. I handed over my American
driver's license, which provoked an even wider smile,
knowledge of my nationality opening a bright green
door onto a world of inflated fines. The Mole produced from one of his many pockets a thick pad and,

reading my name off my license, slowly copied my information onto what was, ostensibly, some sort of official police form.

Czech fines and American fines work along starkly different principles. As almost every American over the age of sixteen knows, minor American infractions take the form of a ticket. The ticket serves as an official record of the violation, and grants the offender time in which to protest their innocence or pay the stipulated amount, a choice so inherently American that most Americans take it for granted. The dual concept that a fine is not paid immediately, but within a certain time frame, and that one can appeal a policeman's judgment to a higher authority is both as natural and intuitive to an American as it is antithetical to a Czech.

The administration of a Czech fine is typically an entirely verbal transaction, with no accompanying paperwork, to be paid immediately and in cash to the policeman requesting it. While such a method obliterates the possibility of an appeal, this system offers one small compensation: haggling. Since the "fine" being levied is going straight into the policeman's pocket, there is no legislated price for freedom. Someone willing to dither can walk away with a relative bargain.

As Dim continued to make a show of scribbling into his pad—though by now he had surely exhausted

the data provided by my license—I expressed to The
Mole in broken Czech my belief that an honest mis-
take such as mine did not merit a fine. I said this in a
friendly, lighthearted manner; interactions with the
Prague police often take on an air of false jollity, as if
everyone is acting in a hastily written play that might
at any moment be called off, but which is never called
off. The Mole assured me in a similarly jovial tone
that mine would not be a large fine like a thousand
crowns (approximately thirty-five dollars—enough
to keep Dim and The Mole in beer for a week), but
a small fine, like three hundred crowns (approximately ten dollars—enough to buy Dim and The
Mole steak dinners). Almost every time The Mole finished speaking, there wavered between us a moment
when it seemed possible that my predicament would
be revealed by The Mole to be a practical joke—there
was no infraction, no fine to pay, in fact he and
Dim weren't even police, they'd found the uniforms
secondhand—but then the moment would dissolve
and The Mole would still be standing there, still
acting like a policeman, and it would be my turn to
speak a line of the parody into which I had been
conscripted.

I responded that three hundred crowns was actually quite big for a fine, which The Mole thought was
a pretty funny thing to say. Once he finished laughing

he asked me whether I was a student or a tourist, and when I told him I was a tourist he became confused. If I was a tourist, he wanted to know, how come I could speak Czech? I explained that I had lived here once, ten years ago, and had returned to visit. Dim had, by this time, stopped writing; I had become too entertaining. Rising to the moment, I told Dim and The Mole that I was a writer.

Have you written a lot of books? The Mole asked, looking impressed, or at least feigning regard.

Only one, I answered, and then, with the help of my Czech–English dictionary, I attempted to explain that I was in Prague in order to write a book about the city. The appearance of the dictionary drew The Mole's attention to the fact that the dictionary was merely one of three books I was carrying, and in an instant he had grabbed all three. Dim and The Mole poked at the books inquisitively, as if not quite sure how they worked.

You are writing a guidebook? The Mole asked.

No, I responded. A book about my thoughts on Prague.

The Mole smiled. This will give you something to write about, he concluded.

By this time the narrow passageway had netted new quarry—a young German woman who, having emerged from the passageway, stopped uncertainly at the sight of Dim and The Mole, who practically cackled at the prospect of doubling their good fortune. While they initiated the same interchange with the German girl as they had with me, it soon became clear that Dim and The Mole's eyes were bigger than their stomachs. They couldn't handle two offenders simultaneously. They flung fractured English at the German, who lobbed her own bewildered English back at them, but they made no motion toward her—that would have meant leaving me unattended, and for reasons obscure to anyone but Dim and The Mole, splitting up was apparently not a possibility. It did not take the German long to ascertain this fact and, as she had yet to be parted from her personal identification, she was able slip to away while Dim, The Mole, and I continued our foray into absurdist street theater.

I do not have three hundred crowns, I lied. In fact I had a couple thousand crowns in my wallet. While I was certainly aware that new infractions might be invented—improper walking shoes or inadequate identification, perhaps—if they intuited this monetary surplus, the amount of the sum Dim and The Mole were requesting was ultimately irrelevant. Even if my fine had been a third as large, I would have protested. There was a principle at stake. Though ten years had passed since I had been an expatriate, I felt I had earned the right to deal with the police in a manner more befitting a Czech, a manner that fell somewhere between wheedling and sport, which most Americans only ever observe in Hollywood comedies.

How much do you have? The Mole asked. I reached into my pocket and produced seventeen crowns. The Mole laughed at the sight of the coins. You can pay two hundred crowns, he offered in a reasonable tone.

This is all I have, I insisted, holding up the flimsy coins.

It is not enough, The Mole shrugged.

Then you will have to come with me until I find a cash machine, I sighed, certain I had just engineered my release. Surely Dim and The Mole would rather relinquish their grip on me than abandon such prime tourist territory, where they were certain of bagging far more compliant trade if they remained. I had not counted on the obvious fact that Dim and The Mole were old hands at harvesting tourists.

There is a cash machine down that street and to the right, The Mole readily answered, helpfully pointing out the route. We will wait for you.

It was a crucial moment, the moment in the script when it became clear who was the victor and who the vanquished. Until that moment I had honestly thought I would be able to walk away unmolested. The Mole was savvier than he let on; he could probably name the nearest ATM from any Prague street corner. I had a brief vision of The Mole's apartment, the water-stained wall over a shoddy, sagging couch decorated with a map of Prague in which each of the city's ATMs was marked with a gold star. I felt betrayed by The Mole's resourcefulness, betrayed by the realization that this wasn't the Hollywood movie I wanted it to be. I whined that it was impossible for me to cross the street since there was no crosswalk. By crossing I would be committing yet another infraction. My petulance did not impress The Mole. And Dim still had my driver's license.

I crossed the street in search of the ATM and, sure enough, there was one exactly where The Mole had said there would be. I withdrew two hundred crowns, hoping it would arrive in one-hundred-crown bills, but instead a single two-hundred-crown bill emerged from the slot, complicating the backup plan I had just concocted.

By the time I returned to the scene of the crime, Dim and The Mole had nabbed two more tourists, an older man and a woman, neither at all clear about why they had been stopped. My return was cause for great excitement between The Mole and Dim and caused The Mole to rush across the street, where I stood waiting to launch my final gambit.

I am a nice girl, I told him. Please, one hundred

crowns only. The Mole smiled and I got the distinct impression this was his favorite part, the part where the mouse pleaded with the raptor. One hundred crowns, I told him, and I'll write about you in my book.

The Mole shook his head. You will write bad things, he said.

No, I assured him. For one hundred crowns I will write good things.

The older couple had crossed the street with The Mole, perhaps thinking they were meant to follow, only to realize that they had been unexpectedly reprieved: The Mole was now far too busy with me to deal with them, and Dim was still on the far side of the street, keeping an eye on the passage as if it might move if he turned his back on it. The couple walked away, waving.

I took out my digital camera. Your picture, I offered.

The Mole made as if to refuse and then coopera-tively posed. As soon as I snapped the shot he was at my side. When his grinning face appeared on the screen he shook his head and grabbed the camera from me, bending down with the camera as if to smash it. I think I knew he was not really going to crush my camera under his boot, but there was a moment when we were no longer on a Prague street: we were in any schoolyard anywhere in the world. The camera had become a hat, a coat, a book, and he the kid who already had hair sprouting above his lip, the bully who trafficked in his own strength. Then the moment passed. The Mole returned my camera to me.

I must consult with my partner, he said. You stay here: it is too dangerous for you to cross the street. Dim still had my driver's license and it occurred to me—in a slight variation on the previous moment's schoolyard scenario—that the two of them could dash through the passageway, laughing. I would never see my license again.

Instead The Mole returned to my side of the street with Dim in tow and informed his partner that I would pay one hundred crowns. The pad into which Dim had been so assiduously writing had vanished. There was no ticket to be issued, just The Mole's waiting palm. I reached into my pocket, produced the two-hundred-crown note, and asked for change. To my utter astonishment The Mole actually took the bill and gave me a hundred-crown note in return.

Here is the nice thing I will say about The Mole, as promised: He was a man of his word.

Dim relinquished my driver's license. I was returning my license to my wallet when The Mole asked me if I was married or single. I didn't understand the question and he repeated, in English, Miss or Mrs.?

Mrs., I told him, as Ms. is not a concept that exists in the Czech Republic. Do you like beer? The Mole asked. Where do you live? he asked.

Goodbye, I said, walking away.

Goodbye, answered The Mole, waving.

Visiting the Dead

KAREL ČAPEK

Vyšehrad Cemetery requires a lengthier metro ride
than most visitors to Prague have time or inclination
to take. Were it more centrally located, its outer walls
would certainly be lined with tour buses, the rows
between its gravestones host to lines of gawking international tourists led by umbrella-wielding guides.
Thankfully Vyšehrad's location to the south of center
city has spared it this fate and its gorgeous, sculptural
headstones are left largely unmolested.

Vyšehrad is one of Prague's treasures. It was originally established at the end of the nineteenth century as the final destination for Prague's cultural elite,
the Czech equivalent of Paris's Montmartre or Père
Lachaise, with the key difference that Vyšehrad's

farthest-flung graves are still within reach of the elongated shadow of its church at sunset. Such smallness breeds intimacy; unlike the famous sprawling cemeteries of Paris, it is possible to spend an hour here and feel acquainted with the place. Vyšehrad's population is a veritable Who's Who of Czech cultural heroes. Among the writers, actors, artists, athletes, scientists, and musicians buried here are Antonín Dvořák, Jan Neruda, Alfhons Mucha, and Karel Čapek. Women are generally subsidiary residents. Though several actresses claim their own headstones along with a few female writers, artists, and musicians, Vyšehrad is largely a society of dead men. A roster outside the cemetery gate lists the notable names and their grave numbers; the unlisted are those who shone less brightly but paid for the privilege of rubbing decaying shoulders with Prague's dead luminaries. As a result almost every headstone reads like a resumé, each inhabitant anxious to prove their worthiness among such lofty company.

Buried among the sculptors, actors, and composers are master builders and professors of otolaryngology, engineers and Czech postal officials. The gravestone of Frank Tetauer asserts his rightful membership by proclaiming him a Ph.D., a writer, a playwright, a critic, and a translator. Below the aforementioned curriculum vitae are four lines of Frank's original poetry on the topic of death and below this—in a single line barely visible—are three words: HIS WIFE ANNA.

Though Frank may have gone a little heavier on the resumé and the poetry than most, his gravestone is by no means unique; the determined careerists interred in Vyšehrad seldom chose to include the word "father" or "husband" on their headstones, and the names of their wives are generally squeezed into whatever space is left over.

Vyšehrad greatly benefits from the fact that many of its tenants died during the first quarter of the twentieth century, when the cemetery was young and Czechoslovakia was a country newly created from the ashes of the Austro-Hungarian empire, a period of national revival that had the aesthetic good fortune of coinciding with the ascendancy of Art Nouveau. The lettering on these markers alone is worth the metro trip: the gravestones are graced with fanciful alphabets ripe with luscious curves and angled serifs.

Because few of Vyšehrad's great artists and great egos were content to settle for a standard gray marble slab upon their demise, Vyšehrad doubles as an out-door sculpture garden. One grave features a life-sized wraithlike sculpture rising from the ground on tiptoe. Another grave features a sculptural trompe l'oeil of startlingly realistic white marble doves, one of which lies draped over the edge of the headstone, its neck broken. Less representational headstones include an abstract metal sculpture suggesting the form of a head-less female angel and an enigmatic organic marble gravestone split by a curved channel. One particularly fanciful grave marker appears to be part wind vane and part cuckoo clock. More conventional tenants opted for busts, generally life-sized, perched atop dark marble columns so that their eyes return the gazes of passersby. Walking between rows of gravestones feels like proceeding down the receiving line of a strangely silent garden party.

Vyšehrad sits on a massive outcropping of rock that towers over the city, and the air in the cemetery is fresher than at the city's center. Many of the grave surfaces have been turned into small gardens, the neat rectangles of soil sporting leafy ground cover, small shrubs, or flowers. Though some graves are better tended than others, none are overgrown or weedy: even on a weekday afternoon it is possible to spot gray-haired family members watering plants and lighting candles. It is peaceful walking among the small rectangular gardens and the proud sculptures, breathing air free from the telltale taint of burning coal that is Prague's bitter trademark during cooler weather. And then, of course, there is the added thrill of being in the presence of famous dead people.

Visiting a famous grave is an odd thing: not only is there no guarantee the dead had any hand in designing their gravestone, but in visiting a famous grave it is likely one is visiting a place the famous person in question never actually saw. But cemeteries have a special relationship with time. For the interred, time has been truly eliminated; the marker above their graves documents the exact moment when, for them, time stopped. A cemetery is a place of quiescence. Unchanging rows of gravestones bestow a sense of stasis upon its visitors, with all evidence to the contrary concealed beneath a thick layer of earth. Busts, photos, and carvings depict faces unmarred by debilitation, disease, or decay. For this reason, just as a widow might visit the grave of her husband to seek comfort, it is possible to visit the grave of an artist who died a century ago and feel as if one is in proximity to a tangible presence.

Visiting a famous grave delivers a thrill of an entirely different order than visiting a famous home. A certain degree of abstract thinking is required when presented with a plaque that reads, "So and so slept here." An empty home cannot help but bestow a sense of absence and abandonment: the impotence of the personal effects of its former inhabitant is inarguable. No matter how artful the arrangement of materials strewn across a desk's surface, it is patently obvious that nothing has happened at that desk for a very long time. The visitor has arrived hopelessly late; the party ended long ago. Not so a gravestone. A grave offers the real goods: not the pen that once was held but the hand itself that wielded it. Never mind that the force that caused the hand to move is long gone and what

lies beneath the ground might not even be recogniz-
able as a hand anymore. The satisfaction of being in
the presence of physical remains is visceral. Certain
native tribes once ate select pieces of their dead in
order to incorporate their good qualities, so that the
dead might continue to live within them. Visiting a
body's resting place is the citified cousin of such an
instinct, bestowing a pale sense of that primal com-
munion. It is as close as people get to baying at the
moon.

The roster beside Vyšehrad's gate indicates that the
celebrated Czech writer Karel Čapek is buried at
grave number 107, a few rows away from Dvořák. The
numbers lead toward the back of the cemetery, just
beyond the church's shadow, but at 107 there is no
evidence of the brilliant individualist who coined the
word "robot" and who created a parodic world in
which humans made war on giant talking newts.
Number 107 is a stranger's grave. A return to the
cemetery gate will not clarify this fact: the roster
clearly identifies Čapek as number 107. Only if a visitor is lucky will she be standing by the gate when an
old Czech man and his grandson walk through the
gate, the grandson peevishly muttering "Karel Čapek,
Karel Čapek" under his breath in a way that suggests
he has been brought here before. These two seasoned
visitors will walk past grave number 107 without a
second glance and proceed toward the last row before

the cemetery wall, a row the uninitiated might well walk down without spotting anything of note. The pair will stop before a cast-iron grave marker in the shape of an open book, Karel Čapek's name formed by delicate lines inscribed on its pages and rendered practically invisible in direct sunlight. Čapek's grave boasts a garden that is more lush than most, covered in purple-leafed plants and dotted with small drooping green buds on the verge of birthing white blossoms. The small numbered marker at the grave's foot clearly reads "47." It is as if by night the cemetery plays a funerary version of musical chairs once the cemetery gates close. The busts of magnates and composers dance cheek to jowl by moonlight, Čapek's open book leaves its designated slot to skim the surface of an Olympic figure skater's obelisk, and the marble doves flutter around the uplifted hands of the wraith, sepulchral shenanigans that do not end by sunrise, forcing their perpetrators to grab the nearest available vacancies, leaving Čapek sixty spaces over from where he had begun.

The act of seeing a name on a grave marker that has previously only graced the spines of books and title pages births a reflexive, physical response: the mouth curves into a grin, the eyes widen, and the heart beats a little faster. This is recognition. It is no different than the response sparked by spotting a familiar face while walking down the street. It is a response unaffected by the fact that Čapek has been dead for over sixty years. He is here: there is his name.

FRANZ KAFKA

Franz Kafka is not buried in Vyšehrad. Nor is he buried in Olšany, which lies in the district of Žižkov, on Prague's southeast perimeter, and which has served as the city's Christian burial ground since the eighteenth century. Gravestones mark the final resting places of gentile professors, city officials, businessmen, and merchants. There are a few scattered busts, but the graves here are far more conventional and plain-spoken than Vyšehrad's. The remains of three centuries of regular citizenry take up five hundred thousand square meters and are divided into thirteen different sections, each representing a different portion of the cemetery's—and the country's—history. Olšany's gravestones reflect Prague's shifting governance across the centuries and function as a granite history book. The oldest section of the graveyard, dating from the days of the Austro-Hungarian empire, is populated with German headstones. With the advent of the country's independence and national awakening in the early 1900s, German-language headstones give way almost entirely to Czech ones. After the 1940s Czech graves begin to admit into their midst the occasional Cyrillic headstone, but these again give way to Czech. Jan Palach, the Czech college student who set fire to himself and became the country's most famous anti-Communist martyr, was originally buried here in 1969, but his body was disinterred and removed from Prague a few years later by wary Communist authorities when his grave became a place of pilgrimage for Czech citizens. His remains were returned to Olšany in 1990.

On a nascent spring day, Olšany is a busy place. The flower shops beside the cemetery entrance are doing a brisk business. A coin-operated machine vending memorial candles just inside the front gate has been emptied. Old ladies arrive in brightly colored coats, carrying bottles of water and dust brooms. They walk with the purpose and confidence of frequent visitors. Weeds are plucked; new flowers are planted; old plants are pruned and watered; marble is swept free of dirt and dust in acknowledgment of winter's approaching end. From the back of one section comes a steady tapping sound, like that of a woodpecker: at a family tomb, a white-haired man in a baseball cap and a down vest carves new names into the stone with a hammer and chisel, his hand gilded with white marble dust. Further on, as her daughter pulls stray weeds a young woman rakes the dirt covering her husband's grave until it resembles a Japanese meditation garden. Above the carved name on the left half of the headstone is a small oval photograph of a man with a moustache. The right half of the headstone is blank. In

Olšany, as in almost any other cemetery, a blank head-stone seems purely practical in nature: the purchaser of a family stone trusts that future deaths will leave bodies to be buried, and people to bury them. But a visit to the cemetery that borders Olšany reveals such a sentiment to be an act of faith, and something that can be betrayed.

The New Jewish Cemetery lies beyond Olšany's eastern edge and is considerably smaller than its neighbor. Its name is a relative term. The New Jewish Cemetery is the granddaughter of the Old Jewish Cemetery, a tiny patch of ground in Old Town that contains twelve thousand gravestones. Marking burials from the fifteenth to the eighteenth centuries, the crumbling stones are lodged one atop the other like dulled teeth within a fossilized jaw. The stones represent only a small fraction of the cemetery's population, which is estimated at a hundred thousand: the bodies are buried one on top of another as deep as twelve layers in obeyance of a Prague law that for centuries forbade Jews from being buried anywhere else.

A hand-painted sign inside the New Jewish Cemetery's front entrance directs visitors along the cemetery's southern wall to Kafka's grave, where he is buried with his mother and father. Because Kafka's demise preceded his parents', his name tops the gravestone, an angular granite obelisk beside which grows a thin pine sapling. Leaning against the stone is a black marble plaque inscribed to the memory of Kafka's three sisters, who died in concentration camps. Dried yellow roses are strewn among the stones that cover the grave. Yellowed notes are tucked among these stones, and these attest to the unique power of a gravesite. People do not leave notes tucked into the floorboards of houses; only at a grave does writing a message to a dead man not seem like a pointless and empty act. And yet, the customary thrill that attends proximity to someone of Kafka's stature is tempered by the cemetery's unrelenting solitude. The attention paid to Kafka's grave—the flowers, the notes, and the skinny pine sapling—only draw further attention to the profound neglect of the hundreds of gravestones surrounding it. Kafka's grave is a lonely place, a place that does not invite lingering.

The history carved into the granite of the New Jewish Cemetery's headstones differs from Olšany's. The majority of the Jewish Cemetery's graves date from the cemetery's establishment in the 1890s to the 1930s. In fact, there exists a century-wide gap between the Old Jewish Cemetery's newest graves, dating from the late 1700s, and the New Jewish Cemetery's oldest ones. A separate Jewish cemetery containing the missing century's graves was once located a few blocks from the New Cemetery, but this other burial ground was turned into a park in the 1970s, after there weren't enough Jews around to complain about its destruction. The truth of this stark fact is borne out through observation. Although the New Jewish Cemetery contains a few scattered graves belonging to Jews who returned to Prague after surviving the insanity of the Second World War, it is difficult to find a gravestone more recent than the 1930s.

The New Jewish Cemetery's opening hours are shorter than Olšany's. The paths between the graves are completely overrun with ivy, such that they are no longer paths but leafy furrows that make walking difficult. Overgrowth submerges shoes at every step. The stillness inside the New Jewish Cemetery is profound. The ivy that covers the pathways has also covered some of the gravestones and climbed the trees. There are no old ladies here, no freshly tended graves. No flower shops stand near its front entrance.

It is a popular misconception that cemeteries are for the dead. Cemeteries serve the living. They provide places to remember and to mourn, to attest to life's larger continuation in the face of smaller ends. A tended cemetery is itself a living creature of earth and candles and flowers. But when there are no living to remember the stories and faces and names of a cemetery's dead, a cemetery dies. In the New Jewish Cemetery family headstones that are largely blank await additions that will never come.

Park Redux

T HE NORTHERN DISTRICT OF HOLEŠOVICE began as a nineteenth-century suburb and is today a largely unremarkable neighborhood of apartment buildings, but along the northward horizon blooms a clock tower, the midsection of which is an open-air spiral staircase that for over a century has stood against the blue sky like a massive strand of dangling DNA. The tower belongs to the grandest building within Výstaviště, the nineteenth-century exhibition grounds that lie along the tram tracks at the northern end of Holešovice. The grounds and buildings were constructed for Prague's 1891 Jubilee Industrial Exhibition, which was the closest the city ever got to hosting a World's Fair. While the clock tower was inspired by Eiffel's slightly earlier Parisian triumph, it tops an expansive wrought-iron and glass exhibition building that combines the onion domes of Greek Orthodoxy, the airiness of classic European train stations, and the whimsy of the pre-modern amusement park. There is no other building like it in all of Prague—Prague architecture, while often beautiful, is never this fun— and on the typically gray days that define Prague's winters the building rises before its viewer like a mirage.

During the turbulent and gloomy century that followed the optimism of Výstaviště's construction, the novelty of the exhibition hall's size probably spared it from falling into decrepitude: large buildings are uncommon enough in Prague that this one proved useful. In the early days of the Communist regime Výstaviště played host to various Communist congresses. With the advent of capitalism it has become Prague's equivalent of a convention center.

Výstaviště also serves as an unlikely boundary between the pre- and post-twentieth-century incarnations of what people think of when they think of the word *park*. In the United States, the traditional park—the green kind—tends to be kept at a safe distance from the kind featuring rollercoasters and bumper cars. Amusement parks lie off highway exit ramps or in back lots behind shopping malls. A respectful distance is maintained between their whir and thump and the green islands that amend urban and suburban grids. But here, Prague mixes its milk with its meat, its dessert with its dinner. West of

Výstaviště lies peaceful Stromovka, a green expanse of trees and paths that for centuries was the private hunting preserve of kings and emperors. East of Výstaviště lies Lunapark, the result of Coney Island being run through a blender, reflected in a funhouse mirror, and roughly translated into Czech.

THE FLOOD OF 2002 subsumed Stromovka Park and now it is a ruined beauty. The sticky mud that once covered everything is gone but the park's trees bear witness to the river's rise: water rings encircling trunks memorialize the river's surreal height. Below the rings the trunks are strangely pale, less the color of bark than the complexion of a convalescent after a long illness.

An old building manifests its longevity in the details of its construction, but an old park hides its age. No signs or plaques announce Stromovka Park's origins. Stromovka's trees are tall and thick-trunked, but neither the trees nor the park's sloping landscape suggests that Stromovka is seven hundred years old. Only Stromovka's recent ruination provides evidence of its antiquity. In the 1500s, the Habsburg emperor Rudolf II transformed Stromovka from a royal park into a hunting preserve, stocking the grounds with four thousand animals and constructing an artificial pond. An underground canal was built to channel river water from the Vltava to feed this imperial fishing hole, an engineering feat ingenious for the sixteenth century and catastrophic for the twenty-first. Holešovice lies opposite the river from the district of Karlín and was not as hard hit by the flood, but Rudolf's underground canal faithfully channeled the Vltava's rising waters into the pond, swallowing the park whole. Six months after the water's subsidence, there is nothing to implicate the pond except the trees: the ones closest to its banks wear the highest water rings.

In the wake of the flood, Stromovka was closed to visitors but now it is once again a place for strolling and a green haven for dogs and children. Old ladies walk the park paths with slow but determined gaits that attest to the unwillingness of Prague's elderly to abdicate independence to arthritis. In March the old ladies come wearing fuzzy hats, their necks warmed by mangy, glass-eyed minks with stiff paws not much smaller than those of the miniature dogs that walk nervously beside them. It is still cold but the snow and ice have melted so the old ladies can walk without fear of frozen patches, their heavy black shoes clomping with cautious confidence against the black asphalt.

Only the old ladies keep their dogs leashed here. Their terriers and Chihuahuas can't compete with Stromovka's true sovereigns. Though dogs are permitted everywhere in the city—including on subways and inside restaurants—in the park they are king. The very idea of a dog run in a Prague park is absurd: in Stromovka, apartment-penned mutts—part Lab, part beagle, part German shepherd, part wolf—frolic un-fettered by fences or leashes. Exuberant butt-sniffing and vestigial pack-forming ensue, but Prague's dog owners shoo their rollicking charges from the park's decaying playground, where young children waddle about in thick pants and coats, only their soft, pink faces exposed to the crisp, coal-tainted air.

Stromovka's playground hasn't been refurbished since its Soviet construction. The surfaces beneath its swings and monkey bars aren't cushiony rubber or even soft grass or sand, but hard-packed dirt. The play-ground's dubious centerpiece is a model Sputnik large enough to hold three toddlers in its hollow center. It is accessed by a metal ladder and exited via a concrete slide, which emerges from Sputnik's far window like a stream of frozen factory sludge. Early March is, per-haps, the ideal time to enjoy the slide's rough, pock-marked surface, for children are still wearing enough layers to descend without decimating their backsides.

To the west of the playground, an abandoned building appears alongside a path without preamble, a seventeenth-century exoskeleton lying discarded like the molted carapace of a baronial beetle. It is distinctly not an urban building—it's too long. Buildings like this weren't designed for city blocks; they were created to reign over open tracts of land. Three stories tall, with a grandly arched ground floor arcade and a recessed second floor circumnavigated by a stone balcony, the edifice resembles something that would be more at home in the French countryside, the moldering estate of a viscount gone to seed. It's the park's decaying equivalent of Výstaviště's exhibition hall, an anomalous fragment of the past projecting itself stubbornly into the present.

The building is the cause célèbre of the Šlechtovy Culture Club. The club's name is hand-painted in red on a piece of scrap wood affixed above the entrance to a makeshift beer garden that neighbors the perimeter fence. The ground here still bears the hallmark of recent flood—the bare earth is not pocked or gullied but is instead almost perfectly smooth, attesting to its recent incarnation as riverbed. Though the flood is months past, here it feels more recent. The Šlechtovy Culture Club feels assembled, spontaneously and triumphantly, from salvaged parts. Inside the dirt compound, a wooden shack sells beer, hot wine, tea, potato chips, and kielbasa. There are a few rough wooden benches and tables, the remains of a spiral staircase, and a gazebo that has seen better days. Šlechtovy's patrons are unfazed when a small pack of dogs rushes into the compound barking loudly, running beneath and around tables and knocking over trash cans. A few loose dogs are nothing compared to a flood, photos of which are attached to the compound's inside fence. One shows the gazebo flooded to its roof. Another shows the compound's seventeenth-century neighbor surrounded by still waters, the ground-floor arcade half-submerged. It is a fairy-tale image, the entire building seemingly rising as if by magic from the center of a peaceful lake.

In a gesture of documentation practically unheard of in a city too awash in history to notate its particulars, a laminated page beside the Šlechtovy Culture Club's flood photos traces the past of its namesake. The building in whose decaying shadow the club stands was originally the imperial hunting lodge of Emperor Leopold I. In the final years of the Austro-Hungarian empire, the building left Habsburg hands and became the Šlechtovy Restaurant, but eventually fell into disrepair. The history ends with this vaguely optimistic sentence: "Ideally the restaurant will be restored in the upcoming years with state funds, and will be rented," which seems to suggest that even its self-appointed historians have their doubts.

Eventually the dogs leave the way they arrived—in a dervish of barking and jumping and lolling tongues. The club's patrons warm their hands on plastic cups of cheap mulled wine, sipping slowly, savoring each swallow. From the vantage point of an uneven wooden bench, Stromovka is a world unto itself: there is no sign of Výstaviště or its unlikely eastern neighbor.

There is only the wine, the recently restored quiet, and this place that exists—half-joke and half-dream—beside a gorgeous ruin of a building older than the American Revolutionary War.

ALONG THE EASTERN FLANK of Stromovka, beyond Výstaviště's exhibition hall, the older version of *park* is separated from the more recent only by an iron fence. Here, birdsong has been replaced by pop music, trees by machines that twirl and spin. The lack of a buffer is disorienting. Standing there feels like violating an obscure but salient natural law.

Even on a drizzly, gray Sunday Czechs come to Lunapark, open no matter what the season, ten crowns during the week, twenty-five on weekends, children under two meters admitted free. Up by the entrance, a neglected glass case beside the ticket window once contained an intact white cardboard scale model of the amusement park, but now the model is largely collapsed, a miniature vision of destruction that recalls Šlechtovy's flood photos. Rising from colored construction paper, the ramshackle cardboard structures are accented by oversized, rough-hewn chunks of spray-painted foam, presumably meant to symbolize absent greenery or massive, nonexistent boulders. An air of melancholy hangs about the ravaged model. Rather than a professional display, the materials and execution suggest a painstakingly assembled extra-credit project that has been trashed by bullies on the way to school. Upon purchasing their tickets visitors bypass the glass display case in favor of Výstaviště's metal entrance gate where, ignoring the cobbled plaza's neo-Baroque splendor, they head straight for Lunapark.

On a Sunday afternoon Lunapark is the realm of small children. Slump-shouldered parents lug strollers up and down stairs. They have no reason to doubt the ubiquity of stairs in amusement parks—there is only one amusement park in Prague and it comes with stairs. Young fathers are clad in fatigues or camouflage caps and exhibit the wariness of Vietnam vets. Young mothers wear either short skirts and knee-high boots or tight jeans and fuzzy coats, the latter outfit only marginally better suited to the weather. Their children run ahead, intent with mission, their hands grasping a ticket or a coin.

Though Lunapark has neighbored Stromovka for over a decade, its rides are the rides of American parking lots and county fairgrounds. Its bumper cars and go-carts and spinning things could be disassembled in a few hours without leaving a trace. Each ride blares music, techno competing with pop competing with Bollywood soundtracks to create an aural traffic accident. On top of this are the carny barkers, who are universally understood no matter what language they speak because carnies say the same thing everywhere: pay to play.

Supplementing Lunapark's rides and games are a smattering of odd-lot attractions that give the impression of having been purchased half-price at some sort of amusement park remnant sale. There is a very small aquarium; a planetarium; a reproduction of the Globe Theater that strives for interior authenticity only, its exterior an ad hoc assemblage of metal brackets and plywood; and a fountain that stands dry save for Friday and Saturday nights, when people buy tickets to watch it light up and burble in time to popular music. Near the fountain is a restaurant that caters to the late-night weekend crowd. A large exterior menu billboard advertises a Freddy Mercury T-bone steak, a Sonny and Cher mixed grill, and a Jimi Hendrix pork cutlet.

In addition to its celebrity meats, the park offers a wide array of discomfiting confections. Sprouted along the park's asphalt paths like strange outcroppings of mushrooms, Lunapark's vendors offer sugar in an alarming array of forms, which they display from booths constructed from metal pipes, wooden tables, and tarps. The sheer number of vendors seems insupportable in a park this size. The booths practically line the walkways, making it clear that sugar is second only to electricity in keeping the park running. Children stand before the tables with the eyes of wolves, their mouths sticky with something just eaten or half-sucked; teenage boys purchase cookies for their girlfriends; exhausted mothers buy themselves a bag of something to make it through another hour of insistent hand-tugging, something to prevent them from collapsing where they stand.

The sweets are divided into three food groups: cookies, cakes, and candies. The cookies and candies are piled across tables in a standing Technicolor invitation to sugar coma, with additional cookies hanging from clotheslines strung along the inside of the tarp. To anyone who once or still possesses a sugar tooth it is difficult not to look at these booths without getting very excited. The sheer variety of options causes the heart to pound. The booths are beautiful despite their rough construction. The various species of sugar are displayed with the care of museum specimens, everything immaculately stacked and arranged by sugar curators, men and women wearing down vests to stave off the lingering cold of winter, presiding over their wares with a bored, proprietary air.

The candies come in cellophane bags and on sticks. There are candied nuts and caramels and foot-long suckers shaped like horns and round red lollipops the size of an infant's head. There are chocolates, and nougats, and obscure objects dusted with sugar bearing indecipherable Czech names on their labels, candies that demand to be tasted to be understood.

Though the cookies are invariably iced gingerbread, the gingerbread assumes such an array of sizes and shapes that it's difficult not to believe a heart-shaped cookie the size of a kitchen plate will taste different from a cell phone cookie, which will differ distinctly from a gangsta Tweety Bird cookie, or one bearing a message to Mom or Grandma, Radka or Petr.

The cakes are less pervasive and more alarming. Like the cookies, the type of cake doesn't vary. Each is a small sponge cake covered in colored marzipan. Some of these take the innocuous forms of apples and bananas and pears, and that's fine—these are shapes marzipan is permitted to assume. It is possible when walking by the cake stands to see nothing amiss among these Old World innocents, marzipan being one of those delicacies that—along with hazelnuts and decent chocolate—has for some strange reason not found equal footing across the Atlantic. But on closer inspection, the oblong brown cakes beside the apples are revealed to be hedgehogs, the pink ones pigs. Beside the pigs are cakes that have been made to resemble cauliflowers, and beside the cauliflowers are light blue, ovular marzipan cakes that have been individually printed with the word VIAGRA. Part of the shock of these objects is that they are handmade. It's one thing to imagine a machine spitting these things out and another to picture a hot kitchen filled with pink-skinned ladies shaping each individual marzipan

Viagra pill with thick, fleshy fingers. The allure of a hedgehog or a piglet to a cake-hungry child is understandable, but cauliflowers and Viagra pills give rise to dogged, unanswerable questions: What were those thick-fingered ladies thinking as they inscribed each blue cake? Who are the cauliflowers for?

An afternoon spent at Lunapark summons a third pressing question, one concerning the average capacity of the Czech bladder. Hundreds of people are here, but there is only one bathroom, located at the very back of the park. It is a corrugated metal shack the yellow of boiled corn. Urinals cost three crowns and stalls cost five crowns, a price that includes a small rectangle of toilet paper torn from its roll by a bathroom attendant whose nose, one can only hope, has become inured to the smell. Unless Czechs have the urinary capacity of camels, there's no way everyone who needs to urinate pays the bathroom lady to do it. The terrible yellow lavatory is too out of the way: the lines fronting it are too short. People must be going behind booths and rides. They must be walking to the fair's edge and going behind bushes, the entire amusement park encircled by a shallow moat of pee.

Such rustic facilities are consistent with the other stray anachronisms that haunt Lunapark, apparitions comparable to Stromovka's imperial hunting lodge. Primary among these is a shooting gallery that wouldn't have looked out of place on the grounds of

Lunapark's Coney Island namesake, which opened for business in 1903. The shooting gallery's hand-cut tin figures are attached to painted tin backdrops in which jungle scenes with exotic animals alternate with village scenes from a pre-mechanized age. There are field laborers, a man in a rowboat, two men on a seesaw, a windmill, and even an interior tableau entitled "Happy Family," in which the successful shooter is rewarded with a vision of a mother rocking a cradle. Each scene is dotted with black tin targets that effect mechanical rewards for precise marksmanship, but constellations of pockmarks stretching across the backdrops and figures attest to untold years of crooked aim.

Coney Island's earliest amusement park contained a carousel, but Prague's retrograde version is even more old-fashioned: a circular open-sided tent edged with ponies that methodically trace the circle's shit-lined perimeter. A man beside the animals wields a stick to keep them moving, but he doesn't need to do much. The ponies know the drill and besides, there's nowhere else for them to go.

The ponies and the shooting gallery may be the only park attractions not adorned with airbrushed women in various states of debauch. Like most of Europe, post-Communist Prague enjoys a relaxed relationship to the female form, but it's strange to see that relationship embodied on amusement park backdrops. Behind a flying dragon ride, a naked blonde kisses a naked blue-skinned brunette with wings and a tail, their bare breasts colliding. The shirtless, cantaloupe-breasted ladies who grace the games of chance sport bikini tan lines and particularly detailed nipples. Steps away from the pre-modern ponies, an airbrushed young lady appears opposite a portrait of Uncle Sam. She is wearing spangles and an American flag and is gleefully sliding her fingers inside her blue satin hot pants. She makes no impression on the Czech tots who run past her to patronize the kiddie roulette wheel. Meanwhile, the ponies continue to tread their circle, providing the sixteenth century an unexpected olfactory foothold in the midst of the twenty-first. Empires rise and fall, ideologies wax and wane, language evolves and words take on new meanings, but the smell of pony dung is forever.

Through a Tram Darkly

O N A FRIDAY NIGHT A CZECH SKA BAND PLAYS to a packed house at the All Baron's Society, a fraternal meeting hall whose walls are lined with portraits of its past members, grave men affecting that universal symbol of fraternity, ridiculous headgear—in this case, feathered pillbox hats. These men are all dead now, the most recent club portrait dating from 1958, when the greenest member doesn't look any younger than fifty. It's probably best they are deceased: they wouldn't have been pleased with tonight's lineup. The ska band has been playing for hours. They've already run through every song they know and are now playing each one a second and third time. Sometimes they sing in Czech, sometimes in English, and sometimes in something in between. The old Czech woman working the coat room is wearing ear plugs and complains that she can still hear the music. Tables line the room's margins but they're empty save for spilled shot glasses, half-empty beer steins, full ashtrays, and coats and sweaters shed by the crowd, who swing and bounce on the dance floor as if they've never heard these songs before, as if the night is just beginning and the set has just begun.

It's impossible to get a drink. There is no bar, just a long hallway leading to an off-limits kitchen. Anyone desiring a drink must stake out the hallway, lie in wait for the club's single waiter to emerge from behind the kitchen door, and then plead with him to take their order. It helps to slip him an advance tip—there are one hundred thirsty people and only one of him. The situation has aroused in the waiter an aggressive strain of apathy native to Prague's overcrowded bars and restaurants. He gives no indication of being able to hear as he presses on with his full tray into the sweat- and smoke-infused air to deliver the last supplicant's drink order, which will be half-spilled by the time it reaches its destination. This is no longer a room in which objects remain upright or stationary: the lead singer is leaning into the microphone at an acute angle that doesn't acknowledge the laws of gravity; in front of the stage, a couple determinedly waltzes to the ska beat; beside them a knot of young Czechs spin on axes determined by innumerable pints of beer and shots of Becherovka.

When the band finally stops there is a melee at the coat check. Everyone pushes into the counter at once: in the absence of music, relocation to some place where the night isn't yet over becomes imperative. The old woman tosses coats indiscriminately across the counter, as eager to be done with their owners as they are to be with her. Down the street is another bar, but it's too jam-packed to allow anyone else through the door; and so it's on to an old mill that has been converted into a bar that can only be reached by crossing a small wooden footbridge over the very Vltava tributary that flooded the place three months earlier. Inside it's crowded but mellow. People lie on couches and smoke joints through white plastic straws. According to the sign on the door the bar closed two hours ago, but drinks are still flowing and no one seems in any hurry to leave. A dog wanders from couch to couch. It is unclear whether he belongs to the bar, to a patron, or whether he just wandered in. He is greeted at each couch with smiles and out-stretched hands. Occasionally a drink is placed before him, but he's a teetotaler who only accepts potato chips. After the mill, the remainder of the night's bars become a seamless blur: the labyrinthine cellar with rooms only large enough to hold one table each; the basement pub in which the smoke is an impregnable curtain obscuring rough wooden picnic tables; the tiny dive where the DJ takes up half the space, leaving no room to dance. When there are no bars left, it's time to go home. It is time to wait for the night tram.

All cities express day and night versions of themselves. By day Prague is tightly contained. Its streetcars fill with responsible citizens who inhabit discrete pockets of space. Conversations are muted. Carefully composed faces glance out windows or stare straight ahead. Old ladies claim seats with imperious authority; and if a car is full, a seat is made available, not just because it's polite but because Prague's grandmas are the arbiters of the city's daylit hours. Their censorious faces attest whether a man's coat is too bright, or a woman's skirt is too short, or a student's behavior so unacceptable that even before she has exited the car she has ceased to exist, having been forcibly exorcised by a granny's gruff gaze.

By day the city combs its hair and wipes its mouth and wears its shirt tucked in, but when the sun goes down, Prague shrugs off its old ladies and steps into something more comfortable. The regular streetcars cease to run and are replaced by less frequent night trams that trace different paths along the city's rails.

The tram is the night's last crowded bar. Even when the evening is warm, its windows are fogged with breath and body heat. The night tram reeks of cigarettes and alcohol and terrible food eaten in bleary defense against a hangover: soggy pizza slices, greasy fried cheese, and stone-cold French fries. These are all the drunk, red-eyed city has left to offer.

Judgment is suspended; the day's dictates have been drowned. People talk and laugh and sometimes sing. Fatigue, giddiness, displeasure, and contentment are all on display, expressions painted by vodka and beer but curated by the night tram. Bodies press against windows. Plastic bucket seats meant for one provide refuge for two as friends and lovers double up to gain more space to breathe. The crush of people is as anonymous as a basement game of Seven Minutes in Heaven. Couples lean into each other with unmasked intent, kissing as if they are alone. Chic disco habitués brush hems with sloppy drunks; a neatly dressed woman reads a French novel, her seated body turned toward the window in a simulation of solitude; a few feet away from her a violently drunk couple argues, their faces contorted with the fathomless betrayal of offended infants. Every night tram contains at least one inebriate slumped in a seat. Bets are taken as to whether or not vomiting will occur in transit. When the tram makes a sudden stop, drooping, drunken heads slam into seat backs without waking.

Each tram stop signals someone's return to the street and walk toward bed. The night tram dispatches without fanfare, abandoning its debarked and debauched to various stages of stumble. Folding its accordion doors behind them, it continues its smooth traverse of the city's dark, slick rails. Through the tram's receding windows, people press into each other as if every moment new secrets are being revealed, secrets those outside the tram will never know. At this hour the night tram is the only bright thing on the street and it can be sad to watch it go. Once the sun rises, the decorous day trams will return. People will once again be gainfully employed. There will be errands to run and classes to attend and appearances to maintain. The night tram will feel like a fib. Until the old ladies go to bed. Until midnight comes.

Acknowledgments

MY PRAGUE WANDERINGS AND RESEARCHES WERE ably abetted by Matt Covey, Heather Mount, Ken Nash, Radka Slaba, Will Tizard, and Lawrence Wells. The *Cadogan Guide to Prague* and *Time Out Prague* were valuable references. Thanks also to Caroline Sincerbeaux, Shauna Toh, and especially to Wendy Schmalz, agent extraordinaire.

This book benefited immensely from the critique and insight of Oliver Broudy, Tim Kreider, and Jason Little.

ABOUT THE AUTHOR

MYLA GOLDBERG lives in Brooklyn, New York, with her husband and daughter. Her second novel, *Wickett's Remedy,* will be published in 2005.

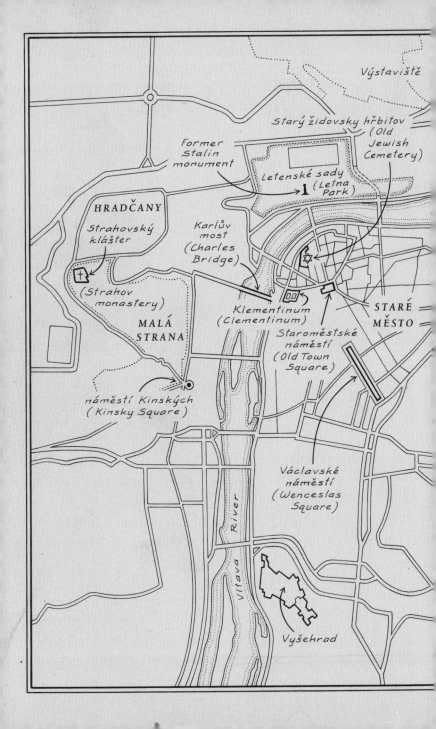

Výstaviště

Starý židovsky hřbitov (Old Jewish Cemetery)

former Stalin monument

Letenské sady (Letna Park)

HRADČANY

Strahovský klášter

Karlův most (Charles Bridge)

(Strahov monastery)

STARÉ MĚSTO

MALÁ STRANA

Klementinum (Clementinum)

Staroměstské náměstí (Old Town Square)

náměstí Kinských (Kinsky Square)

Václavské náměstí (Wenceslas Square)

Vltava River

Vyšehrad